iPhone
The Missing Manual

iPhone: The Missing Manual   BY DAVID POGUE

Published by O'Reilly Media, Inc., 1005 Gravenstein Highway North, Sebastopol, CA 95472.

O'Reilly books may be purchased for educational, business, or sales promotional use. Online editions are also available for most titles *(safari.oreilly.com)*. For more information, contact our corporate/institutional sales department: 800.998.9938 or *corporate@oreilly.com*.

Executive Editor: Laurie Petrycki

Copy Editors: Teresa Noelle Roberts, Nan Barber

Proofreader: Nan Barber

Indexer: David Pogue

Cover Designers: Randy Comer, Karen Montgomery, Phil Simpson, and Suzy Wiviott

Interior Designer: Phil Simpson (based on a design by Ron Bilodeau)

Print History:

August 2007:   First Edition.

ISBN-10: 0-596-51374-7
ISBN-13: 978-0-596-51374-0
[F]   [07/07]

Contents

Part 2: The iPhone as iPod

Part 3: The iPhone Online

The Missing Credits

David Pogue (author, indexer) is the weekly tech columnist for the *New York Times*, an Emmy-winning correspondent for *CBS News Sunday Morning*, 2006 winner of an Online News Association award (for online commentary), and the creator of the Missing Manual series. He's the author or co-author of 42 books, including 17 in this series and six in the *"For Dummies"* line (including *Macs, Magic, Opera*, and *Classical Music*). In his other life, David is a former Broadway show conductor, a magician, and a pianist.

News, photos, links to his columns and weekly videos await at *www.davidpogue. com.* He welcomes feedback about his books by email at *david@pogueman. com.*

J.D. Biersdorfer (iTunes, syncing, and accessories chapters) is the author of *iPod: The Missing Manual* and co-author of *The Internet: The Missing Manual* and the second edition of *Google: The Missing Manual.* She has been writing the weekly computer Q&A column for the *New York Times* since 1998, and has covered everything from 17th-century Indian art to the world of female hackers. Her work has appeared in *Rolling Stone, The New York Times Book Review,* and the *AIGA Journal of Graphic Design.* Biersdorfer, who studied theater at Indiana University, now lives in New York City and is equally obsessed with the BBC and the banjo. Email: *jd.biersdorfer@gmail.com.*

Acknowledgments

The Missing Manual series is a joint venture between the dream team introduced on these pages and O'Reilly Media. I'm grateful to all of them, and also to a few people who did massive favors for this book.

Teresa Noelle Roberts gave the manuscript a delightful copy-editing makeover. I was thrilled to be reunited with my original Missing Manuals editor Nan Barber, who copy-edited some chapters and proofread the whole thing. And working with designer Phil Simpson on this book was a blast, as it has been now for 30 books in a row.

My gratitude also goes to photographer Tim Geaney, graphics goddess Lesa Snider King, and my cheerful intern Zach Brass; they helped me hammer away at the problem of capturing what's on the iPhone screen. Brian Jepson bailed me out of technical underbrush more than once. Apple's Greg Joswiak, Bob Borchers, Natalie Kerris, Jennifer Bowcock, and Mark Brunst donated valuable time to my cause—right in the middle of the iPhone launch.

Thanks, too, to the readers and fans who submitted delicious tips, inspired only by a desire to help their fellow iPhoners (and get a free book).

A few people undertook days-long special efforts to make this book the best it could be. They included Rich Koster, who, as the book's beta reader, helped to improve it in a hundred different ways (sorry, Rich, there's no room to mention your Web site, *http://disneyecho.emuck.com*). Bill Oakey spent a whole weekend helping me solve the "two-mailbox problem" (page 139) and other technical email issues. And Chris Vincent, with determination and talent, went the extra *several* miles to solve a rather key production problem. Their involvement was a highlight of the book-creation process.

Thanks to David Rogelberg for believing in the idea, and above all, to Jennifer, Kelly, Tia, and Jeffrey, who make these books—and everything else—possible.

—*David Pogue*

The Missing Manual Series

Missing Manual books are superbly written guides to computer products that don't come with printed manuals (which is just about all of them). Each book features a handcrafted index; cross-references to specific page numbers (not just "See Chapter 14"); and RepKover, a detached-spine binding that lets the book lie perfectly flat without the assistance of weights or cinder blocks. Recent and upcoming titles include:

- *Windows Vista: The Missing Manual* by David Pogue

- *Mac OS X: The Missing Manual,* Leopard Edition by David Pogue

- *Windows XP Home Edition: The Missing Manual,* by David Pogue

- *Windows XP Pro: The Missing Manual,* by David Pogue, Craig Zacker, and L.J. Zacker

- *Photoshop CS3: The Missing Manual* by Colin Smith

- *Access 2007: The Missing Manual* by Matthew MacDonald

- *CSS: The Missing Manual* by David Sawyer McFarland

- *Creating Web Sites: The Missing Manual* by Matthew MacDonald

- *Digital Photography: The Missing Manual* by Chris Grover, Barbara Brundage

- *Dreamweaver CS3: The Missing Manual* by David Sawyer McFarland

- *Flash CS3: The Missing Manual* by E. A. Vander Veer and Chris Grover

- *eBay: The Missing Manual* by Nancy Conner

- *Excel 2007: The Missing Manual* by Matthew MacDonald

- *FileMaker Pro 8: The Missing Manual* by Geoff Coffey and Susan Prosser

- *FrontPage 2003: The Missing Manual* **by Jessica Mantaro**

- *Google: The Missing Manual,* 2nd Edition by Sarah Milstein and Rael Dornfest

- *Home Networking: The Missing Manual* by Scott Lowe

- *The Internet: The Missing Manual* by David Pogue and J.D. Biersdorfer

- *iPod: The Missing Manual,* **5th Edition** by J.D. Biersdorfer

- *PCs: The Missing Manual* by Andy Rathbone

- *Photoshop Elements 5: The Missing Manual* by Barbara Brundage

- *PowerPoint 2007: The Missing Manual* by Emily A. Vander Veer

- *QuickBooks 2006: The Missing Manual* by Bonnie Biafore

- *Word 2007: The Missing Manual* by Chris Grover

- *Switching to the Mac: The Missing Manual*, Tiger Edition by David Pogue

- *AppleScript: The Missing Manual* by Adam Goldstein

- *AppleWorks 6: The Missing Manual* by Jim Elferdink and David Reynolds

- *GarageBand 2: The Missing Manual* by David Pogue

- *iLife '05: The Missing Manual* by David Pogue

- *iMovie 6 & iDVD: The Missing Manual* by David Pogue

- *iPhoto 6: The Missing Manual* by David Pogue and Derrick Story

- *iWork '05: The Missing Manual* by Jim Elferdink

- *Office 2004 for Macintosh: The Missing Manual* by Mark H. Walker, Franklin Tessler, and Paul Berkowitz

- *iPhone: The Missing Manual* by David Pogue

For Starters

The "For Starters" books contain just the most essential information from their larger counterparts—in larger type, with a more spacious layout, and none of those advanced sidebars. Recent titles include:

- *Windows Vista for Starters: The Missing Manual* by David Pogue

- *Windows XP for Starters: The Missing Manual* by David Pogue

- *Access 2007 for Starters: The Missing Manual* by Matthew MacDonald

- *Excel 2007 for Starters: The Missing Manual* by Matthew MacDonald

- *Quicken 2006 for Starters: The Missing Manual* by Bonnie Biafore

- *Word 2007 for Starters: The Missing Manual* by Chris Grover

- *PowerPoint 2007 for Starters: The Missing Manual* by Emily A. Vander Veer

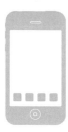

Introduction

Y ou can say the iPhone is everything it was supposed to be, or you can say it wasn't worth the hype. But one thing's for sure: It was the most eagerly awaited new gadget in consumer-electronics history. In the six months from when Apple announced the iPhone to the day it went on sale, the phone was written up in 12,000 print articles and 69 million Web pages. At the flagship Fifth Avenue Apple store in New York, people began lining up for the iPhone *five days* before the thing went on sale. (Well, one guy did.)

Remember how mystified everyone was when Apple called its music player the iPod—instead of, say, iMusic or iSongs or something? The reason was that Apple had much bigger plans for the iPod—photos, videos, documents, and so on. Maybe the company should have saved that name for the iPhone. This thing goes so far beyond "phone," the name almost does it a disservice.

The iPhone, of course, is not just a phone. It's an iPod too, with 4 or 8 gigabytes of storage (enough for about 850 or 1,850 songs) and the biggest, highest resolution screen in iPod history. And it's the best Internet terminal you've ever seen on a phone. It doesn't display text-only email headers and bare-bones, stripped-down Web pages; it shows fully formatted email (with attachments, thank you) and displays real Web sites with fonts and design intact.

It's also a calendar, address book, calculator, alarm clock, stopwatch, stock tracker, real-time traffic reporter, RSS reader, and weather forecaster. It even stands in for a flashlight and, with the screen turned off, a pocket mirror.

And that's before you get into the Pleasure Factor: the way the thing fits in your hand; the gorgeous, animated software that's both sophisticated and drop-dead simple to operate.

Not too shabby for a 1.0 product, eh?

About This Book

By way of a printed guide to the iPhone, Apple provides only a fold-out leaf-let. It's got a clever name—Finger Tips—but to learn your way around, you're expected to use an electronic PDF document. This PDF covers the basics well, but it's largely free of details, hacks, workarounds, tutorials, humor, and any acknowledgment of the iPhone's flaws. You can't mark your place, underline, or read it in the bathroom.

The purpose of this book, then, is to serve as the manual that should have accompanied the iPhone.

Writing computer books can be an annoying job. You commit something to print, and then *bam*—the software gets updated or revised, and suddenly your book is out of date.

That will happen to this book especially. The iPhone is a *platform*. It's a com-puter, so Apple can update and improve it by sending it new software bits. Apple will issue new programs to fill those empty spaces at the bottom of the Home screen, fix bugs, and patch holes in the feature list. To picture where the iPhone will be five years from now, just look at how much better, sleeker, and more powerful today's iPod is than the original 2001 black-and-white brick.

Those updates, and the online community of hackers, programmers, acces-sory makers, and fans, are just getting started. Therefore, you should think of this book the way you think of the first iPhone: as a darned good start. This book will be updated by free, periodic email newsletters as developments unfold. To get them, register this book at *www.oreilly.com*. (Here's a shortcut to the registration page: *http://tinyurl.com/yo82k3.*)

About the Outline

iPhone: The Missing Manual is divided into six parts, each containing several chapters:

- Part 1, **The iPhone as Phone,** covers everything related to phone calls: dialing, answering, voicemail, conference calling, text messaging, and the Contacts (address book) program.

- Part 2, **The iPhone as iPod,** is dedicated to the iPhone's ability to play back photos, music, podcasts, movies, and TV shows. This section also covers the iPhone's built-in camera.

- Part 3, **The iPhone Online,** is a detailed exploration of the iPhone's third talent: its ability to get you onto the Internet, either over a Wi-Fi hot spot connection or via AT&T's cellular network. It's all here: email, Web browsing, YouTube, Google Maps, RSS, weather, stocks, and so on.

- Part 4, **Beyond iPhone,** describes the world beyond the iPhone itself—like the copy of iTunes on your Mac or PC that's responsible for filling up the iPhone with music, videos, and photos, and syncing the calendar, address book, and mail settings. These chapters also offer a look at the exploding world of add-on, Web-based software for the iPhone, and accessories like chargers, car adapters, and carrying cases. It wraps up with a tour of the iPhone's control panel—the Settings program.

- Part 5, **Appendixes,** contains two reference chapters. Appendix A walks you through the setup and signup process, in which you activate your phone, choose a calling plan, and find out your phone number. Appendix B is a master compendium of troubleshooting, maintenance, and battery information.

About→These→Arrows

Throughout this book, and throughout the Missing Manual series, you'll find sentences like this one: Tap Home→Settings→Wi-Fi. That's shorthand for a much longer instruction that directs you to open three nested screens in sequence, like this: "Press the iPhone's Home button. On the Home screen, tap Settings; on the Settings screen, tap Wi-Fi."

Similarly, this kind of arrow shorthand helps to simplify the business of choosing commands in menus, like File→Print.

About MissingManuals.com

To get the most out of this book, visit *www.missingmanuals.com*. Click the "Missing CD-ROM" link, and then click this book's title to reveal a neat, organized, chapter-by-chapter list of the shareware and freeware mentioned in this book.

But the Web site also offers corrections and updates to the book (to see them, click the book's title, and then click Errata). In fact, please submit such corrections and updates yourself! In an effort to keep the book as up-to-date and accurate as possible, each time we print more copies of this book, we'll make any confirmed corrections you've suggested. We'll also note such changes on the Web site, so you can mark important corrections into your own copy of the book, if you like. And we'll keep the book current as Apple releases more iPhone updates.

1 The Guided Tour

I f you had never seen all the videos and photos of the iPhone, and you just found It lying on someone's desk, you might not guess that it's a phone (let alone an iPod/Web browser/alarm clock/stopwatch/etc.). You can't see any antenna, mouthpiece, earpiece—and, goodness knows, there are no number keys for dialing.

It's all there, though, hidden inside this sleek black-and-silver slab.

For the rest of this book, and for the rest of your life with the iPhone, you'll be expected to know what's meant by, for example, "the Home button" and "the Sleep/Wake switch." A guided tour, therefore, is in order. Keep hands and feet inside the tram at all times.

Sleep Switch (On/Off)

On the top edge of the iPhone, you'll find a black plastic button shaped like a dash.

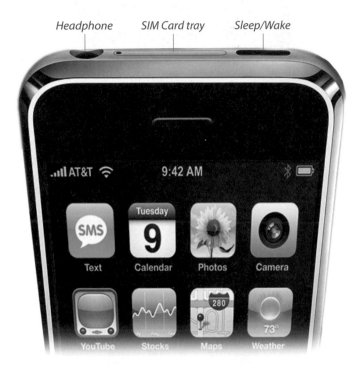

This button has several functions.

- **Sleep/Wake.** Tapping it once puts the iPhone to sleep—that is, into Standby mode, ready for incoming calls but consuming very little power. Tapping it again turns on the screen, so it's ready for action.

- **On/Off.** This switch can also turn the iPhone off completely, so it consumes no power at all; incoming calls get dumped into voicemail (page 53). You might turn the iPhone off whenever you're not going to use it for a few days.

  To turn the iPhone off, press the Sleep/Wake switch for three seconds. The screen changes to say, "slide to power off." Confirm your decision by placing a fingertip on the red right-pointing arrow and sliding to the right. The device shuts off completely.

To turn the iPhone back on, press the switch again for a couple seconds. The chromelike Apple logo appears as the phone boots up.

- **Answer call/Dump to voicemail.** The upper-right switch has one more function. When a call comes in, you can tap it *once* to silence the ringing or vibrating. After four rings, the call goes to your voicemail.

    You can also tap it *twice* to dump the call to voicemail immediately. (Of course, because they didn't hear four rings, iPhone veterans will know that you've blown them off. Bruised egos may result. Welcome to the new world of iPhone Etiquette.)

Locked Mode

When you don't touch the screen for one minute, or when you put the iPhone to sleep, the phone *locks* itself. When it's locked, the screen isn't touch-sensitive. Fortunately, you can still take phone calls and control music playback.

Remember, this phone is all touch screen, so it's much more prone to accidental button-pushes than most phones. You wouldn't want to discover that your iPhone has been calling people or taking photos from the depths of your pocket or purse.

That's why the first thing you do after waking the iPhone is *unlock* it. Fortunately, that's easy (and a lot of fun) to do: place your fingertip on the gray arrow and slide it to the right, as indicated by the animation.

> **Tip** The iPhone can demand a password each time it wakes up, if you like. See page

SIM Card Slot

On the top edge of the phone, in the middle, is a tiny pinhole next to what looks like a very thin slot cover (see page 6). If you push a pin or an unfolded paper clip straight into the hole, the SIM card tray suddenly pops out.

So what's a SIM card?

It turns out that there are two major cellphone network types: *CDMA*, used by Verizon and Sprint; and *GSM*, used by AT&T, T-Mobile, and most other countries around the world. Your iPhone works only on GSM networks. (That's one huge reason that Apple chose AT&T as its exclusive carrier. Apple wanted to design a phone that works overseas.)

Every GSM phone keeps your account information—details like your phone number and calling-plan details—on a tiny memory card known as a SIM card (Subscriber Information Module). On some phones, though not the iPhone, it even stores your address book.

What's cool is that, by removing the card and putting it into *another* GSM phone, you transplant the iPhone's brain. The other phone now knows your number and account details, which can be handy when your iPhone goes in for repair or battery replacement.

Apple thinks that SIM cards are geeky and intimidating, and that they should be invisible. That's why, unlike most GSM phones, your iPhone came with the card preinstalled and ready to go. Most people will never have any reason to open this tray, unless they just want to see what a SIM card looks like.

 Note You can't use any other company's SIM card in the iPhone—it's not an "unlocked" GSM phone. Other recent AT&T cards will work, however, but only after you first activate them. After inserting the other card — it fits only one way, with the AT&T logo facing up—connect the iPhone to your computer and let the iTunes software walk you through the process.

If you were curious enough to open it up, you close the tray simply by pushing it back into the phone until it clicks.

Audio Jack

The tour continues with the top-left corner of the iPhone. Here's where you plug in the white earbuds that came with your iPhone.

This little recessed hole is no ordinary 3.5-millimeter audio jack, however. It contains a secret fourth pin that conducts sound *into* the phone from the microphone on the earbuds cord. Now you, too, can be one of those executives who walk down the street barking orders to nobody in particular. The iPhone can stay in your pocket as you walk or drive. You hear the other person through your earbuds, and the mike on the cord picks up your voice.

Incidentally, the tiny microphone nodule on the cord is more than a microphone; it's also an Answer/Hang Up clicker. See page 32 for the full scoop.

 Tip In theory, you can use any standard headphones with the iPhone — a welcome bit of news for audiophiles who don't think the included earbuds do their music justice.

The catch, however, is that the molding around the iPhone's audio jack prevents most miniplugs from going all the way in. You may be able to get your headphones to fit by trimming its own plastic collar with a razor blade—or you can spend $10 for a headphone adapter (from Belkin.com, among others) to get around this problem.

The Screen

The touch screen is your mouse, keyboard, dialing pad, and note pad. It's going to get fingerprinty and streaky, although it wipes clean with a quick rub on your sleeve. You can also use it as a mirror when the iPhone is off.

 Note Geeks may enjoy knowing that the screen is 320 by 480 pixels.

But what about scratches? Fortunately, Apple learned its lesson on this one. The iPhone screen is made of optical-quality, chemically treated glass—not polycarbonate plastic like the iPod's screen. It's actually very difficult to scratch glass; try it on a window pane some day.

If you're nervous about protecting your iPhone, you can always get a carrying case for it. But in general, the iPhone is far more scratch-resistant than the iPod. Even many Apple employees carry the iPhone in their pockets without carrying cases.

 Tip Camouflaged behind the black glass above the earpiece, where you can't see them except with a bright flashlight, are two sensors. First, there's an ambient-light sensor that brightens the display when you're in sunlight and dims it in darker places. You can also adjust the brightness manually; see page 246.

Second, there's a proximity sensor. When something (like your head) is close to the sensor when you're using the phone functions, it shuts off the screen illumination and touch sensitivity. Try it out with your hand. (It works only in the Phone application.) You save power and avoid tapping buttons with your cheekbone.

Screen Icons

Here's a roundup of the icons that you may see in the status bar at the top of the iPhone screen, from left to right.

- **.ıll Cell Signal.** As on any cellphone, the number of bars indicates the strength of your cell signal, and thus the quality of your call audio and likelihood of losing the connection. If there are zero bars, the dreaded words "No service" appear here.

- **E EDGE Network.** When this logo appears, your iPhone can get onto the Internet via AT&T's very handy, but very slow, EDGE cellular network (page 106). In general, if you have a cell signal, you also have an EDGE signal.

- **✈ Airplane Mode.** If you see the airplane instead of signal and Wi-Fi bars, the iPhone is in Airplane mode (page 110).

- **⦿ Wi-Fi Signal.** When you're connected to a wireless Wi-Fi Internet hot spot (page 106), this indicator appears. The more "soundwaves," the stronger the signal.

- **🔒** The iPhone is locked—meaning that the screen and most buttons don't work, to avoid accidental presses—whenever it goes to sleep. See page 7.

- **2:34 PM.** When the iPhone is unlocked, a digital clock replaces the Lock symbol. To set the clock, see page 249.

- **▶** Play indicator. The iPhone's playing music. Before you respond, "well, duh!," keep in mind that you may not be able to hear the music playing. For example, maybe the earbuds are plugged into the iPhone but aren't in your ears. So this icon is actually a handy reminder that you're running your battery down unnecessarily.

- ⏰ **Alarm.** You've got an alarm set. This reminder, too, can be valuable, especially when you intend to sleep late and don't *want* an alarm to go off. See page 249 for setting (and turning off) alarms.

- ✳ **Bluetooth connection.** The iPhone is connected wirelessly to a Bluetooth earpiece or hands-free car system, as described on page 188. (If this symbol is gray, it means that Bluetooth is turned on—and draining your battery—but it's not connected to any other gear.)

- ▦ **TTY symbol.** You've turned on Teletype mode, meaning that the iPhone can communicate with a Teletype machine. (That's a special machine that lets deaf people make phone calls by typing and reading text. It hooks up to the iPhone with a special cable that Apple sells from its Web site.)

- ▱ **Battery meter.** When the iPhone is plugged into its cradle (which is itself plugged into a wall outlet or computer), the lightning bolt appears, indicating that the phone is charging. Otherwise, the battery logo "empties out" from right to left to indicate how much charge remains.

Home Button

Here it is. The one and only *real* button on the front of this phone. Push it to summon the Home screen, which is your gateway to everything the iPhone can do.

Having a Home button is a wonderful thing. It means you can never get lost. No matter how deeply you burrow into the iPhone software, no matter how far off track you find yourself, one push of the Home button takes you all the way back to the beginning.

Sounds simple, but remember that the iPhone doesn't have an actual Back button or End button. The Home button is the *only* way out of some screens.

The Home button also wakes up the iPhone if it's in Standby mode. That's sometimes easier than finding the Sleep/Wake switch on the top edge.

 Tip The Home button is also a "force quit" button. If you press it for six seconds straight, whatever program you're running completely shuts down. That's a good troubleshooting technique when a particular program seems to be acting up.

Some beginners forget that the Home button is a physical pushbutton—it's not touch-sensitive like the screen—and get frustrated when it doesn't respond. Give it a real manly push.

Silencer Switch, Volume Keys

Praise be to the gods of technology—this phone has a Silence All switch!

This little flipper, on the left edge at the top, means that no ringer or alert sound will humiliate you in a meeting, a movie, or church. When you move the switch toward the front of the iPhone, the ringer is on. When you push it toward the back, exposing the orange dot, the ringer is off.

 Tip Even when silenced, the iPhone still makes noise if you've explicitly set an alarm, as described on page 188.

Also, the phone still vibrates when the silencer is engaged, although you can turn this feature off; see page 245.

Silent/Ring switch

Volume up

Volume down

No menus, no holding down keys, just instant silence. All cellphones should have this feature.

Below the silencer, still on the left edge, is the volume control—an up/down rocker switch. It works three different ways:

- On a call, these buttons adjust the speaker or earbud volume.

- When you're listening to music, they adjust the playback volume.

- At all other times, they adjust the volume of sound effects like the ringer and alarms.

Either way, a corresponding volume graphic appears on the screen to show you where you are on the volume scale.

The Bottom and the Back

On the bottom edge of the iPhone, Apple has parked three important components, none of which you'll ever have to bother with: the speakerphone speaker, the microphone, and the 30-pin connector that charges and syncs the iPhone with your computer.

Microphone

Speaker

On the back of the iPhone, the camera lens (page 100) appears in the upper-left corner. The rest of the back is *mostly* textured aluminum—all except the bottom, which is black plastic. That's where the antenna is. Cellphone signals have a hard time going through metal, which is why this one piece is made of plastic. Fortunately for people who fear cellphone radiation, the antenna is as far from your brain as it can be.

Camera

Not a self-portrait mirror

Note You may have noticed one standard cellphone feature that's *not* here: the battery compartment door.

The battery isn't user-replaceable. It's *rechargeable*, of course—it charges whenever it's in the white dock—but after 300 or 400 charges, it will start to hold less juice. Eventually, you'll have to pay Apple to install a new battery (page 277). (Apple says that the added bulk of a protective plastic battery compartment, a removable door and latch, and battery retaining springs would have meant a much smaller battery—or a much thicker iPhone.).

In the Box

Inside the minimalist box, you get the iPhone, its earbud/mike cord, and:

- **The charging/syncing dock.** You charge your iPhone by seating it in this white desktop dock. Most people plug the dock's USB cord into a Mac or PC for simultaneous syncing and charging. (See Chapter 11.)

- **The AC adapter.** When you're traveling without a computer, though, you can plug the dock's USB cable into the included two-prong outlet adapter, so you can charge the iPhone directly from a wall socket.

- **Finger Tips.** Cute name for a cute fold-out leaflet of iPhone basics.

- **Two white Apple decals.** Let your car window show that you're a phone-carrying member of the Apple cult.

- **A screen cloth.** This little pseudo-suede cloth wipes the grease off the screen, although your clothing does just as well.

What you *won't* find in the box (because it wouldn't fit) is a CD containing the iTunes software. You're expected to have a copy of that on your computer already. In fact, you *must* have an iTunes account to set up and use the iPhone (Appendix A).

If you don't have iTunes on your computer, you can download it from *www. apple.com/itunes*.

Seven Basic Finger Techniques

The iPhone isn't quite like any machine that came before it, and operating it isn't quite like using any other machine. You do everything on the touch screen instead of with physical buttons. Here's what you need to know.

Tap

You'll do a lot of tapping on the iPhone's on-screen buttons. They're usually nice and big, giving your fleshy fingertip a fat target.

You can't use a stylus, fingernail, pen tip, or anything else; only skin contact works. That's too bad for people who wear gloves on the job.

Drag

When you're zoomed into a map, Web page, email, or photo, you scroll around just by sliding your finger across the glass in any direction—like a flick, but slower and more controlled. It's a huge improvement over scroll bars, especially when you want to scroll diagonally.

Slide

In some situations, you'll be asked to confirm an action by *sliding* your finger across the screen. That's how you unlock the phone's buttons after it's been in your pocket, for example. It's ingenious, really; you may bump the touch screen when you reach into your pocket for something, but it's extremely unlikely that your knuckles will randomly *slide* it in just the right way.

You also have to swipe to confirm that you want to turn off the iPhone, to answer a call on a locked iPhone, or to shut off an alarm. Swiping like this is also a great shortcut for deleting email or text message.

Flick

A *flick* is a fast, less controlled *slide.* You flick vertically to scroll lists on the iPhone. You'll discover, usually with some expletive like "Whoa!" or "Jeez!," that scrolling a list in this way is a blast. The faster your flick, the faster the list spins downward or upward. But lists have a real-world sort of momentum; they slow down after a second or two, so you can see where you wound up.

At any point during the scrolling of the list, you can flick again (if you didn't go far enough) or tap to stop the scrolling (if you see the item you want to choose).

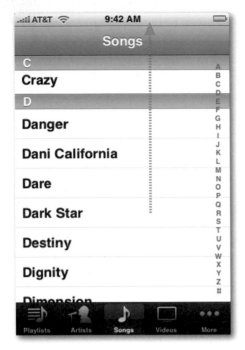

Pinch and Spread

In the Photos, Mail, Web, and Google Maps programs, you can zoom in on a photo, message, Web page, or map by placing two fingers (usually thumb and forefinger) on the glass and spreading them. The image magically grows, as though it's printed on a sheet of rubber.

Once you've zoomed in like this, you can then zoom out again by putting two fingers on the glass and pinching them together.

> **Note** The English language has failed Apple here. Moving your thumb and forefinger closer together has a perfect verb: *pinching*. But there's no word to describe moving them the opposite direction.
>
> Apple uses the oxymoronic expression *pinch out* to describe that move (along with the redundant-sounding *pinch in*). In this book, the opposite of "pinching" is "spreading."

Double-Tap

Double-tapping is actually pretty rare on the iPhone. It's not like the Mac or Windows, where double-clicking the mouse always means "open." Because the iPhone's operating system is far more limited, you open something with *one* tap.

A double tap, therefore, is reserved for three functions:

- In Safari (the Web browser), Photos, and Google Maps programs, double-tapping zooms in on whatever you tap, magnifying it.

- In the same programs, as well as Mail, double-tapping means, "restore to original size" after you've zoomed in.

- When you're watching a video, double-tapping switches *aspect ratios* (video screen shape); see page 83.

Two-Finger Tap

This weird little gesture crops up only in one place: in Google Maps. It means "zoom out." To perform it, you tap once on the screen—with *two* fingers.

The Keyboard

Very few iPhone features have triggered as much angst, hope, and criticism as the on-screen keyboard. It's true, boys and girls: the iPhone has no physical keys. A virtual keyboard, therefore, is the only possible system for entering text.

The keyboard appears automatically whenever you tap in a place where typing is possible: in an outgoing email or text message, in the Notes program, in the address bar of the Web browser, and so on.

Just tap the key you want. As your finger taps the glass, a "speech balloon" appears above your finger, showing an enlarged version of the key you actually hit (since your finger is now blocking your view of the keyboard).

In darker gray, surrounding the letters, you'll find these special keys:

- **Shift (⇧).** When you tap this key, it glows white, to indicate that it's in effect. The next letter you type appears as a capital. Then the ⇧ key automatically returns to normal, meaning that the next letter will be lowercase.

The iPhone has a Caps Lock feature, but you have to request it. In the Settings program, turn on "Enable caps lock" as described on page 252.

From now on, if you double-tap the ⇧ key, the key turns blue. You're now in Caps Lock mode, and you'll now type in ALL CAPITALS until you tap the ⇧ key again. (If you can't seem to make Caps Lock work, try double-tapping the ⇧ key *fast*.)

- **Backspace (⌫).** This key actually has three speeds.

  Tap it once to delete the letter just before the blinking insertion point.

  Hold it down to "walk" backward, deleting as you go.

  If you hold down the key long enough, it starts deleting *words* rather than letters, one whole chunk at a time.

  . Tap this button when you want to type numbers or punctuation. The keyboard changes to offer a palette of numbers and symbols. Tap the same key—which now says ABC—to return to the letters keyboard. (Fortunately, there's a much faster way to get a period; see page 24.)

  Once you're on the numbers/symbols pad, a new dark gray button appears, labeled #+=. Tapping it summons a *third* keyboard layout, containing the less frequently used symbols, like brackets, the # and % symbols, bullets, and math symbols.

- **Return.** Tapping this key moves to the next line, just as on a real keyboard.

Note There's no Tab key in iPhone land, and no Enter key.

Making the Keyboard Work

Some people have no problem tapping those tiny virtual keys; others struggle for days. Either way, here are some tips:

- Don't be freaked out by the tiny narrow keys. Apple *knows* that your fingertip is fatter than that.

  So as you type, use the whole pad of your finger or thumb. Go ahead—tap as though you're trying to make a fingerprint. Don't try to tap with only a skinny part of your finger to match the skinny keys. You'll be surprised at how fast and accurate this method is. (Tap, don't press.)

- This may sound like California New-Age hooey, but **trust** the keyboard. Don't get hung up on individual letters, pausing to check the result, and so on. Just plow on.

- Start out with one-finger typing. Two-thumb, BlackBerry-style typing usually comes much later. You'll drive yourself crazy if you start out that way.

- If you make a mistake, don't reflexively go for the Backspace key (⌫). Instead, just beneath the word you typed, you'll find the iPhone's proposed replacement. The software analyzes the letters **around** the one you typed and, more often than not, figures out what you really meant. For example, if you accidentally type **imsame**, the iPhone realizes that you meant **insane**, and suggests that word.

  To accept its suggestion, tap the Space bar or any piece of punctuation, like a period or question mark.

  To ignore the suggestion, tap it with your finger.

- The suggestion feature can be especially useful when it comes to contractions, which are normally clumsy to type because you have to switch to the punctuation keyboard to find the apostrophe.

So you can save time by *deliberately* leaving out the apostrophe in contractions like *I'm*, *don't*, *can't*, and so on. Type *im*, *dont*, *cant*, and so on. The iPhone proposes *I'm, don't,* or *can't,* so you can just tap the Space bar to fix the word and continue.

Tip But what about contractions like "he'll," "we'll," and "we're?" If you leave out the apostrophe on *these* words, you get "hell," "well," and "were," which are legitimate words—and the iPhone won't correct them!

Solution: Double the last letter. If you type *helll, welll,* and *weree,* the iPhone will suggest "he'll," "we'll," and "we're."

- The suggestion feature also kicks in when the iPhone thinks it knows how you intend to complete a *correctly* spelled word. For example, if you type *fathe*, the suggestion says *father*. This trick usually saves you only a letter or two, but that's better than nothing.

Tip Although you don't see it with your eyes, the sizes of the keys on the iPhone keyboard are actually changing all the time. That is, the software enlarges the "landing area" of certain keys, based on probability.

For example, suppose you type *tim*. Now, the iPhone knows that no word in the language begins *timw* or *timr*—and so, invisibly, it enlarges the "landing area" of the E key, which greatly diminishes your chances of making a typo on that last letter. Cool.

- Without cursor keys, how are you supposed to correct an error that you made a few sentences ago? Easy—use the Loupe.

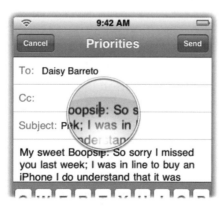

Hold your fingertip down anywhere in the text until you see the magnified circle appear. Without lifting your finger, drag anywhere in the text; you'll see that the insertion point moves along with it. Release when the blinking line is where you want to delete or add text, just as though you'd clicked there with a mouse.

> **Tip** In the Safari address bar, you can skip the part about waiting for the loupe to appear. Once you've clicked into the address, just start *dragging* to make it appear at once.

- Don't bother using the Shift key to capitalize a new sentence. The iPhone does that capitalizing automatically. (To turn this feature on or off, tap Home→Settings→General→Keyboard→Auto-Capitalization.)

How to Type Punctuation with One Touch

On the iPhone, the punctuation keys and alphabet keys appear on two different keyboard layouts. That's a *serious* hassle, because each time you want a period or a comma, it's an awkward, three-step dance: (1) Tap the **?123** key to get the punctuation layout. (2) Tap the period. (3) Tap the ABC key, or just press the Space bar, to return to the alphabet layout.

Imagine how excruciating it is to type, for example, "a P.O. Box in the U.S.A."! That's 34 finger taps and 10 mode changes!

Fortunately, there's a secret way to get a period, comma, or another punctuation mark with only a *single* finger gesture.

The iPhone doesn't register most key presses until you *lift* your finger. But the Shift and Punctuation keys register their taps on the press *down* instead.

So here's what you can do, all in one motion:

❶ **Touch the ?123 key, but don't lift your finger.** The punctuation layout appears.

❷ **Slide your finger a onto the period or comma key, and release.** The ABC layout returns automatically. You've typed a period or a comma with one finger touch instead of three.

> **Tip** If you're a two-thumbed typist, you can also hit the **?123** key with your left thumb, and then tap the punctuation key with your right. It even works on the **#+=** sub-punctuation layout, although you'll probably visit that screen less often.

In fact, you can type any of the punctuation symbols the same way. This technique makes a *huge* difference in the usability of the keyboard.

> **Tip** This same trick saves you a finger-press when capitalizing words, too. You can put your finger down on the ⇧ key and slide directly onto the letter you want to type its uppercase version.

How the Dictionary Works

The iPhone has an English dictionary built in (minus the definitions). As you type, it compares what you've typed against the words in that dictionary (and against the names in your address book). If it finds a match or a partial match, it displays a suggestion just beneath what you've typed.

If you tap the Space bar to accept the suggestion, wonderful.

If you don't—if you dismiss the suggestion and allow the "mistake" to stand—then the iPhone adds that word to a custom, dynamic dictionary, assuming that you've just typed some name, bit of slang, or terminology that wasn't in its dictionary originally. It dawns on the iPhone that maybe that's a legitimate word it doesn't know—and adds it to the dictionary. From now on, in other words, it will accept that bizarre new word as a legitimate word—and, in fact, will even *suggest* it the next time you type something like it.

Words you've added to the dictionary actually *age*. If you stop using some custom term, the iPhone gradually learns to forget it. That's handy behavior if you never intended for that word to become part of the dictionary to begin with (that is, it was a mistake).

 Tip If you feel you've really made a mess of your custom dictionary, and the iPhone keeps suggesting ridiculous alternate words, you can always start fresh. Tap Home→Settings→General→Reset; then tap Reset Keyboard Dictionary. Now the iPhone's dictionary is the way it was when it came from the factory, without any of the words it learned from you.

Charging the iPhone

The iPhone has a built-in, rechargeable battery that fills up a substantial chunk of the iPhone's interior. How long one charge can drive your iPhone depends on what you're doing—music playback saps the battery least, Internet and video sap it the most. But one thing is for sure: Sooner or later, you'll have to recharge the iPhone. (For most people, that's every other day or so.)

You recharge the iPhone by seating it in the white syncing cradle that came with it. You can plug the far end into either of two places to supply power:

- **Your computer's USB jack.** Just make sure that the Mac or PC won't go to sleep or turn off while the iPhone is plugged into it. Not only will the battery not charge, but it may actually *lose* charge if the computer isn't turned on.

- **The AC adapter.** The little white two-prong cube that came with the iPhone snaps onto the end of the cradle's USB cable and plugs into a standard power outlet.

If the iPhone is unlocked, the battery icon in the upper-right corner displays a lightning bolt to let you know that it's receiving electricity and charging the battery. If it's locked, pressing the Home button wakes it long enough to show you a battery gauge big enough to see from space.

In general, you can use the iPhone while it's charging. The one exception: If the battery charge is really low, it may have to soak in several minutes' worth of power before it can turn on.

Battery Life Tips

The biggest wolfers of electricity on your iPhone are its screen and its wireless features. Therefore, you can get substantially longer life from each battery charge by using these features:

- **Dim the screen.** In bright light, the screen brightens (but uses more battery power). In dim light, it darkens.

 Note This works because of an ambient light sensor that's hiding behind the glass above the earpiece. Apple says that it tried having the light sensor active all the time, but it was weird to have the screen constantly dimming and brightening as you used it. So the sensor now samples the ambient light and adjusts the brightness only once—when you unlock the phone after waking it.

You can use this information to your advantage. By covering up the sensor as you unlock the phone, you force it into a low-power, dim screen setting (because the phone believes that it's in a dark room). Or by holding it up to a light as you wake it, you get full brightness. In both cases, you've saved all the taps and navigation it would have taken you to find the manual brightness slider in Settings (page 246).

- **Turn off Wi-Fi.** Tap Home→Settings→Wi-Fi→On/Off. If you're not in a wireless hot spot anyway, you may as well stop the thing from using its radio.

  Or, at the very least, tell the iPhone to stop *searching* for Wi-Fi networks it can connect to. Page 242 has the details.

- **Turn off the phone, too.** In Airplane mode, you shut off both Wi-Fi and the cellular radios, saving the most power of all. Page 110 has details.

2 Phone Calls

A s you probably know, using the iPhone means choosing AT&T Wireless as your cellphone carrier. If you're a Verizon, Sprint, or T-Mobile fan, too bad. AT&T (formerly Cingular) has the iPhone exclusively at least until 2012.

Why did Apple choose AT&T? For two reasons.

First, because Apple wanted a GSM carrier (page 8). Second, because of the way the cellphone world traditionally designs phones. It's the carrier, not the cellphone maker, that wears the pants, makes all the decisions, and wields veto power over any feature. That's why so much traditional cellphone software is so alike—and so terrible.

On this particular phone, however, Apple intended to make its own decisions, and so it required carte-blanche freedom to maneuver. AT&T agreed to let Apple do whatever it liked—without even knowing what the machine was going to be! AT&T was even willing to rework its voicemail system to accommodate Apple's Visual Voicemail idea (page 53).

In fact, to keep the iPhone under Apple's cloak of invisibility, AT&T engineering teams each received only a piece of it so that nobody knew what it all added up to. Apple even supplied AT&T with a bogus user interface to fake them out!

Making Calls

Suppose you've already activated your phone (Appendix A), and the "number of bars" logo in the upper-left corner tells you that you've got cellular reception. You're ready to start a conversation.

Well, *almost* ready. The iPhone offers four ways to dial, but all of them require that you first be in the Phone *application* (program).

To get there:

❶ If you're not already on the Home screen, press the Home button.
You arrive at the Home screen.

❷ Tap the Phone icon. It's always in the lower-left corner of the Home screen.

Tip The tiny circled number in the upper-right corner of the Phone icon tells you how many waiting voicemail messages you have. See page 53.

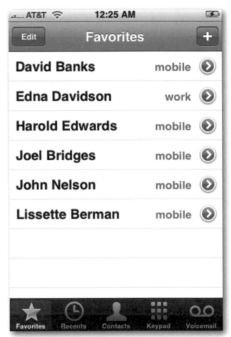

Now you've arrived in the Phone program. A new row of icons appears at the bottom, representing the four ways of dialing:

- **Favorites list.** Here's the iPhone's version of speed-dial keys: It lists the 20 people you think you most frequently call. Tap a name to make the call. (For details on building and editing this list, see page .)

- **Recents list.** Every call you've made, answered, or missed recently appears in this list. Missed callers' names appear in red lettering, which makes them easy to spot—and easy to call back.

Tap a name or number to dial. Or tap the button to view the details of a call—when, where, how long—and, if you like, to add this number to your Contacts list.

- **Contacts.** Your master phone book. If your social circle is longer than one screenful, you'll have the distinct pleasure of *flicking* through it (page 17).

  Or, if you're in a hurry to get to the T's, use the A to Z index down the right edge of the screen. You can tap the last-name initial letter you want (R, or W, or whatever). Alternatively, you can drag your finger up or down the index. The list scrolls in real time.

  In any case, when you see the name you want, tap it to open its "card," filled with phone numbers and other info. Tap the number you want to dial.

  To edit the Contacts list, see page 44.

> How would you like your phonebook sorted alphabetically: by last name or by first name? And how would you like the names to appear: as "Potter, Harry" or as "Harry Potter"? The iPhone lets you choose. See page 255.

- **Keypad.** This dialing pad may be virtual, but the buttons are a *heck* of a lot bigger than they are on regular cellphones, making them easy to tap, even with fat fingers. You can punch in any number and then tap Call to place the call.

Once you've dialed, no matter which method, either hold the iPhone up to your head, put in the earbuds, turn on the speakerphone (page 14), or put on your Bluetooth earpiece—and start talking!

Answering Calls

When someone calls your iPhone, you'll know it; three out of your five senses are alerted. Depending on how you've set up your iPhone, you'll *hear* a ring, *feel* vibration, and *see* the caller's name and photo fill that giant iPhone screen. (Scent and taste will have to wait until iPhone 2.0.)

> **Note** For details on choosing a ring sound (ringtone) and Vibrate mode, see page 245. And for info on the Silence All switch, see page 12.

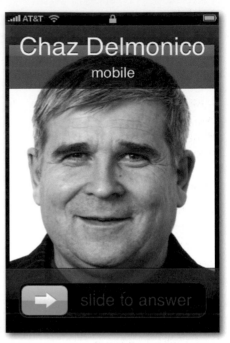

How you answer depends on what's happening at the time:

- **If you're using the iPhone,** tap the green Answer button. Tap End Call when you both have said enough.

- **If the iPhone is asleep or locked,** the screen lights up and says, "slide to answer." If you slide your finger as indicated by the arrow, you simultaneously unlock the phone and answer the call.

- **If you're wearing earbuds,** the music nicely fades out and then pauses; you hear the ring both through the phone's speaker and through your earbuds. Answer by squeezing the clicker on the right earbud cord, or by using either of the methods described above.

    When the call is over, you can click again to hang up—or just wait until the other guy hangs up. Either way, the music will fade in again and resume from precisely the spot where you were so rudely interrupted.

 Incoming calls pause and fade video playback the same way. In this case, though, hanging up does not make video playback resume. Instead, the screen displays the list of videos. Apple says it's a bug in version 1.0.

Multitasking

Don't forget, by the way, that the iPhone is a multitasking master. Once you're on the phone, you can dive into any other program—to check your calendar, for example—without interrupting the call.

If you're connected to the Internet via a Wi-Fi hot spot (page 106), you can even surf the Web, check your email, or use other Internet functions of the iPhone without interrupting your call. (If you're not in a hot spot, you won't be able to get online until the call is complete.)

Silencing the Ring

Sometimes, you need a moment before you can answer the call; maybe you need to exit a meeting or put in the earbuds, for example. In that case, you can stop the ringing and vibrating by pressing one of the physical buttons on the edges (Sleep/Wake button or either volume key). The caller still hears the phone ringing, and you can still answer it within the first four rings, but at least the sound won't be annoying those around you.

(This assumes, of course, that you haven't just flipped the ring-silencing switch, as described on page 12.)

Not Answering Calls

And what if you're listening to a *really* good song, or you see that the call comes from someone you *really* don't want to deal with right now?

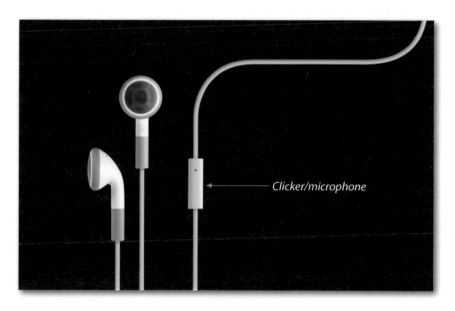

Clicker/microphone

In that case, you have two choices. First, you can just ignore it. If you wait long enough (four rings), the call will go to voicemail (even if you've silenced the ringing/vibrating as described above).

Second, you can dump it to voicemail *immediately* (instead of waiting for the four rings). How you do that depends on the setup:

- **If you're using the iPhone,** tap the Decline button that appears on the screen.

- **If the iPhone is asleep or locked,** tap the Sleep/Wake button twice fast.

- **If you're wearing the earbuds,** squeeze the microphone clicker for two seconds.

Of course, if your callers know you have an iPhone, they'll also know that you've deliberately dumped them into voicemail—because they won't hear all four rings.

Fun with Phone Calls

Whenever you're on a call, the iPhone makes it pitifully easy to perform stunts like turning on the speakerphone, putting someone on hold, taking a second call, and so on. Each of these is a one-tap function.

Here are the six options that appear on the screen whenever you're on a call.

Mute

Tap this button to mute your own microphone, so that the other guy can't hear you. (You can still hear him, though.) Now you have a chance to yell upstairs, to clear the phlegm from your throat, or to do anything else you'd rather the other party not hear. Tap again to unmute.

Keypad

Sometimes, you absolutely have to input touch tones, which is generally a perk only of phones with physical dialing keys. For example, that's usually how you operate home answering machines when you call in for messages, and it's often required by automated banking, reservations, and similar systems.

Tap this button to produce the traditional iPhone dialing pad, illustrated on page 50. Each digit you touch generates the proper touch tone for the computer on the other end to hear.

When you're finished, tap Hide Keypad to return to the dialing-functions screen, or tap End Call if your conversation is complete.

Speaker

Tap this button to turn on the iPhone's built-in speakerphone—a great hands-free option when you're caught without your earbuds or Bluetooth headset. (In fact, the speakerphone doesn't work if the earbuds are plugged in or a Bluetooth headset is connected.)

When you tap the button, it turns blue to indicate that the speaker is activated. Now you can put the iPhone down on a table or counter and have a conversation with both hands free. Tap Speaker again to channel the sound back into the built-in earpiece.

 Remember that the speaker is on the bottom edge. If you're having trouble hearing it, and the volume is all the way up, consider pointing the speaker toward you, or even cupping one hand around the bottom to direct the sound.

Add Call (Conference Calling)

The iPhone is all about software, baby, and that's nowhere more apparent than in its facility for handling multiple calls at once. The simplicity and reliability of this feature puts other cellphones to shame. Never again, in attempting to answer a second call, will you have to tell the first person, "If I lose you, I'll call you back."

Suppose you're on a call. Now then, here's how you can:

- **Make an outgoing call.** Tap Add Call. The iPhone puts the first person on hold—neither of you can hear each other—and returns you to the Phone program and its various phone-number lists. You can now make a second call just the way you made the first. The top of the screen makes clear that the first person is still on hold as you talk to the second.

- **Receive an incoming call.** If a second call comes in while you're on the first, you see the name or number (and photo, if any) of the new caller. You can tap either *Ignore* (meaning, "Send to voicemail; I'm busy now"), *Hold Call + Answer* (the first call is put on hold while you take the second), or *End Call + Answer* (ditch the first call).

 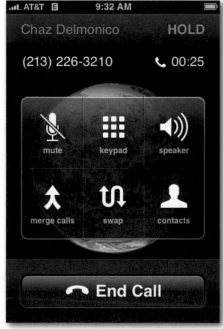

Whenever you're on two calls at once, the top of the screen identifies both other parties. Two new buttons appear, too:

- **Swap** lets you flip back and forth between the two calls. At the top of the screen, you see the names or numbers of your callers. One says HOLD (the one who's on hold, of course) and the other bears a white telephone icon, which lets you know who you're actually speaking to.

  Think how many TV and movie comedies have relied on the old "Woops, I hit the wrong Call Waiting button and now I'm bad-mouthing somebody directly to his face instead of behind his back" gag! That can't happen on the iPhone.

  You can swap calls by tapping Swap or by tapping the HOLD person's name or number.

- **Merge** combines the two calls so all three of you can converse at once. Now the top of the screen announces, "Bill O'Reilly & Al Franken" (or whatever the names of your callers are), and then changes to say "Conference".

  If you tap the ⊙ button, you see the names or numbers of everyone in your conference call. You can drop one of the calls by tapping its ⊙ button (and then End Call to confirm), or choose Private to have a person-

to-person private chat with one participant. (Tap Merge Calls to return to the conference call.)

 Note If a call comes in while you're already talking to someone, tap the "Hold Call + Answer" button. Then tap Merge Calls if you want to add the newcomer to the party.

This business of combining calls into one doesn't have to stop at two. At any time, you can tap Add Call, dial a third number, and then tap Merge to combine it with your first two. And then a fourth call, and a fifth. With you, that makes six people on the call.

Then your problem isn't technological, it's social, as you try to conduct a meaningful conversation without interrupting each other.

 Note Just remember that if you're on the phone with five people at once, you're using up your monthly AT&T minutes five times as fast. Better save those conference calls for weekends!

Hold

When you tap this button, you put the call on hold. Neither you nor the other guy can hear anything. Tap again to resume the conversation.

Contacts

This button opens the address book program, so that you can look up a number or place another call.

Editing the Contacts List

Remember that there are four ways to dial: Favorites, Recents, Contacts, and Keypad.

The Contacts list isn't the first icon in the row at the bottom of the Phone screen. But it's worth describing first, because it's the source from which all other lists spring.

Contacts is your address book—your master phone book. Every cellphone has a Contacts list, of course, but the beauty of the iPhone is that you don't have to type in the phone numbers one at a time. Instead, the iPhone sucks in the entire phone book from your Mac or PC; page 218 has the details.

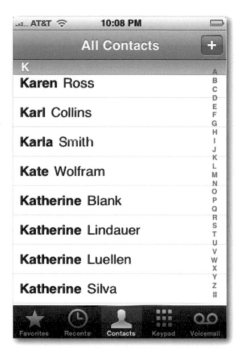

It's infinitely easier to edit your address book on the computer, where you have an actual keyboard and mouse. The iPhone also makes it very easy to add someone's contact information when they call, email, or send a text message to your phone, thanks to a prominent Add to Contacts button.

But if in a pinch, on the road, at gunpoint, you have to add, edit, or remove a contact manually, here's how to do it.

❶ **On the Contacts screen, tap the ✚ button in the upper-right corner.**
   You arrive at the New Contact screen, which teems with empty boxes for phone numbers, email addresses, and so on.

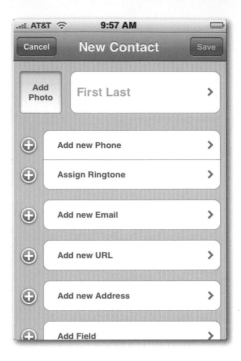

❷ **Tap the First Last box.** The onscreen keyboard opens automatically, ready for typing.

❸ **Type the person's name.** See page 20 for a refresher on using the iPhone's keyboard. Tap each field (First, Last, Company) before typing into it. The iPhone capitalizes the first letter of each name for you.

❹ **Tap the Save button in the upper-right corner.** You return to the New Contact screen.

> **Tip** On the iPhone, buttons that mean "Save," "OK," or "Done" always appear in a blue box, where they're easy to spot.

❺ **Tap "Add new Phone."** The Edit Phone screen appears.

❻ **Type in the phone number, with area code.** If you need to insert a pause—a frequent requirement when dialing access numbers, extension numbers, or voicemail passwords—type the # symbol, which introduces a two-second pause in the dialing. You can type several to create longer pauses.

❼ **Then tap the box below the phone number (which starts out saying "mobile") to specify what _kind_ of phone number it is.** The Label screen offers you a choice of mobile, home, work, main, home fax, pager, and so on.

> **Tip** If that's not enough choice of labels—if, for example, you're entering your friend's yacht phone—tap Add Custom Label at the bottom of the label screen. You're offered the chance to type in a new label. Tap Save when you're done.

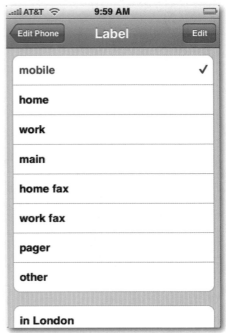

❽ **Tap Save. Repeat steps 5 and 6 to enter additional phone numbers for this person.** If you want to input the person's email address, Web site address (URL), and so on, work your way down the New Contact screen in a similar pattern.

❾ **Add a photo of the person, if you like.** Tap Add Photo. If you have a photo of the person in the iPhone already, tap Choose Existing Photo. You're taken to your photo collection, where you can find a good head-shot (Chapter 5).

Alternatively, tap Take Photo to activate the iPhone's built-in camera (page y). Frame up the person, then tap the green camera button to snap the shot.

In either case, you wind up with the Move and Scale screen. Here, you can frame up the photo so that the person's face is nicely sized and centered. Spread two fingers to enlarge the photo; drag your finger to move the image within the frame. Tap Set Photo to commit the photo to the address book's memory.

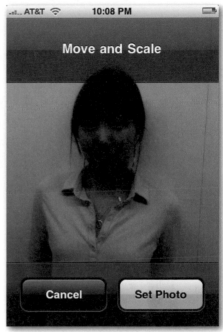

From now on, this photo will pop up on the screen whenever the person calls.

⑩ **Choose a ringtone.** The iPhone lets you choose a different ringtone for each person in your address book. The idea is that you'll know by the sound of the ring who's calling. To do that, tap Assign Ringtone. On the next screen, tap the sound you want and then tap Info to return to the main contact screen.

⑪ **Add an email address, Web address (URL), if you like.** Each has its own button. You add this information just the way you add phone numbers.

⑫ **Add your own fields.** Very cool: If you tap Add Field at the bottom of the screen, you go down the rabbit hole into Field Land, where you can add any of ten additional info bits about the person whose card you're editing: Prefix (like Mr. or Mrs.), Suffix (like M.D. or Esq.), Nickname, Job Title, and so on. Tap Save when you're finished.

 Note To delete any of these information bits later, tap the ⊖ button next to it, and then tap the red Delete button to confirm.

Adding a Contact on the Fly

There's actually another way to add someone to your Contacts list—a faster, on-the-fly method that's more typical of cellphones. Start by bringing the phone number up on the screen:

- Tap Home, then Phone, then Keypad. Dial the number, and then tap the **+👤** button.

- You can also add a number that's in your Recents (recent calls) list, storing it in Contacts for future use. Tap the ❯ button next to the name.

In both cases, finish up by tapping Create New Contact (to enter this person's name for the first time) or Add to Existing Contact (to add a new phone number to someone's existing card that's already in your list). Off you go to the Contacts editing screen shown on page 40.

Editing Someone

To make corrections or changes, tap the person's name in the Contacts list. In the upper-right corner of the Info card, tap Edit.

You return to the screens described above, where you can make whatever changes you like. To edit a phone number, for example, tap it and change away. To delete a number (or any other info bit), tap the ⊖ button next to it, and then tap Delete to confirm.

Deleting Someone

Truth is, you'll probably *add* people to your address book far more often than you'll *delete* them. After all, you meet new people all the time—but you delete people primarily when they die, move away, or break up with you.

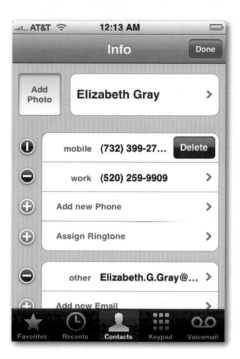

To zap someone, tap the name in the Contacts list and then tap Edit. Next, scroll to the bottom of the screen, tap Delete Contact, and finally confirm by tapping Delete Contact again.

Favorites List

Truth is, you may not wind up dialing much from Contacts. That's the master list, all right, but it's too unwieldy when you just want to call your spouse, your boss, or your lawyer. The iPhone doesn't have any speed-dial buttons, of course, but it does have Favorites—a short, easy-to-scan list of the people you call most often.

You can add names to this list in either of two ways:

- **From the Contacts list.** Tap a name to open the Info screen, where you'll find a button called Add to Favorites. (This button appears only if there is, in fact, a phone number recorded for this person—as opposed to just an email address, for example.) If there's more than one phone number on the Info screen, you're asked to tap the one you want to add to Favorites.

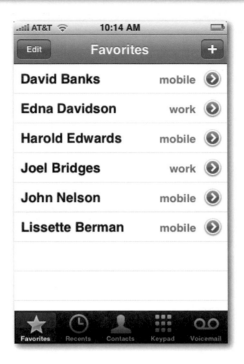

- **From the Recents list.** Tap the button next to any name or number in the Recents list (see the facing page). If it's somebody who's already in your Contacts list, you arrive at the Call Details screen, where one tap on "Add to Favorites" does what it says.

  If it's somebody who's not in Contacts yet, you'll have to *put* them there first. Tap Create New Contact, and then proceed as described on page 40. After you hit Save, you return to the Call Details screen so you can tap Add to Favorites.

The Favorites list holds 20 numbers, max. Once you've added that many, the Add to Favorites and **+** buttons disappear.

Deleting from Favorites

To delete somebody from your Favorites—the morning after a nasty political argument over drinks, for example—tap Edit. Then follow the usual iPhone deletion sequence: First tap the ⊖ button next to the unwanted entry, and then tap Remove to confirm.

Reordering Favorites

Tapping that Edit button at the top of the Favorites list offers another handy feature, too: It lets you drag names up and down, so the most important people appear at the top of the list. Just use the right-side "grip strip" as a handle to move entire names up or down the list.

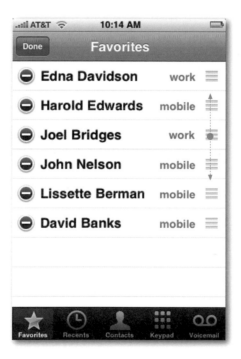

Recents List

Like any self-respecting cellphone, the iPhone maintains a list of everybody you've called or who's called you recently. The idea, of course, is to provide you with a quick way to call someone you've been talking to lately.

To see the list, tap Recents at the bottom of the Phone application. You see a list of the last 75 calls that you've received or placed from your iPhone, along with each person's name or number (depending on whether that name is in Contacts or not) and the date of the call.

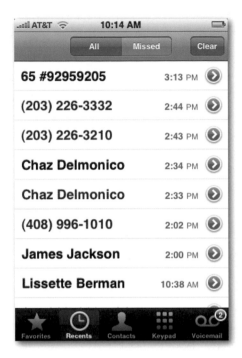

Here's what you need to know about the Recents list:

- Calls that you missed (or sent to voicemail) appear in red type. If you tap the Missed button at the top of the screen, you see *only* your missed calls. All of this color-coding and separate listings is designed to make it easy for you to return calls that you missed, or to try again to reach someone who didn't answer when you called.

- To call someone back—regardless of whether you answered or dialed the call—tap that name or number in the list.

- Tap the ⊙ button next to any call to open the Call Details screen. At the top of the screen, you can see whether this was an Outgoing Call, Incoming Call, or Missed Call.

  What else you see here depends on whether or not the other person is in your Contacts list.

If so, the Call Details screen displays the person's whole information card. For outgoing calls, blue type indicates which of the person's numbers you dialed. A star denotes a phone number that's also in your Favorites list.

If the call *isn't* from someone in your Contacts, you get to see a handy notation at the top of the Call Details screen: the city and state where the calling phone is registered.

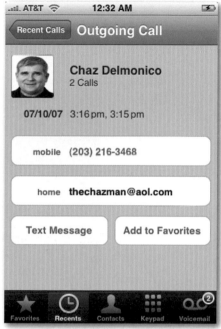

- To save you scrolling, the Recents list thoughtfully combines consecutive calls to or from the same person. If some obsessive ex-lover has been calling you every ten minutes for four hours, you'll see "Chris Meyerson (24)" in the Recents list. (Tap the ⦿ button to see the exact times of the calls.)

- To erase the entire list, thus ruling out the chance that a coworker or significant other might discover your illicit activities, tap Clear at the top of the screen. You'll be asked to confirm your decision. (There's no way to delete individual items in this list.)

The Keypad

The last way to place a call is to tap the Keypad button at the bottom of the screen. The standard iPhone dialing pad appears. It's just like the number pad on a normal cellphone, except that the "keys" are much bigger and you can't feel them.

To make a call, tap out the numbers—use the ⌫ key to backspace if you make a mistake—and then tap the green Call button.

You can also use the keypad to enter a phone number into your Contacts list, thanks to the little +👤 icon in the corner. See page 44 for details.

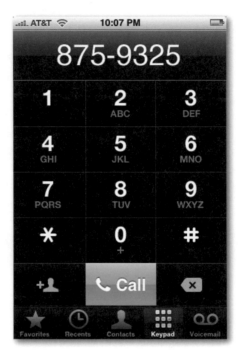

Overseas Calling

The iPhone is a *quad-band GSM* phone, which is a fancy way of saying it also works in any of the 200 countries of the world (including all of Europe) that have GSM phone networks. Cool!

But AT&T's international roaming charges will cost you anywhere from 60 cents to $5 per minute. Not so cool!

If you, a person in Oprah's tax bracket, are fine with that, then all you have to do is remember to call AT&T before you travel. Ask that they turn on the international roaming feature. (They can do that remotely. It's a security step.)

Then off you go. Now you can dial local numbers in the countries you visit, and receive calls from the U.S. from people who dialed your regular number, with the greatest of ease. You can even specify which overseas cell carrier you want to carry your calls, since there may be more than one that's made roaming agreements with AT&T.

See page 243 for details on specifying the overseas carrier. And see *www.wireless. att.com/learn/international/long-distance* for details on this roaming stuff.

If you're *not* interested in paying those massive roaming charges, however, you might want to consider simply renting a cellphone when you get to the country you're visiting.

 Note The iPhone can even add the proper country codes automatically when you dial U.S. numbers; see page 255.

As for calling overseas numbers *from* the U.S., the scheme is simple:

- **North America (Canada, Puerto Rico, Caribbean).** Dial 1, the area code, and the number, just like any other long-distance call.

- **Other countries.** Dial 011, the country code, the city or area code, and the local number. How do you know the country code? Let Google be your friend.

 Tip Instead of dialing 011, you can just hold down the 0 key. That produces the + symbol, which means 011 to the AT&T switchboard.

These calls, too, will cost you. If you do much overseas calling, therefore, consider cutting the overseas-calling rates down to the bone by using Jajah.com. It's a Web service that cleverly uses the Internet to conduct your call—for 3 cents a minute to most countries, vs. 11 cents from the phone company.

You don't have to sign up for anything. Just go to *www.jajah.com* on your iPhone. Fill in your phone number and your overseas friend's, and then click Call.

In a moment, your phone will ring—and you'll hear your friend saying hello. *Neither of you* actually placed the call—Jajah called both of you and connected the calls—so you save all kinds of money. Happy chatting!

3 Fancy Phone Tricks

Once you've savored the exhilaration of making phone calls on the iPhone, you're ready to graduate to some of its fancier tricks: voicemail, sending text messages, using AT&T features like Caller ID and Call Forwarding, and using a Bluetooth headset or car kit.

Visual Voicemail

Without a doubt, Visual Voicemail is one of the iPhone's big selling points. On the iPhone, you don't *dial in* to check for answering-machine messages people have left for you. You don't enter a password. You don't sit through some Ambien-addled recorded lady saying, "You have...17...messages. To hear your messages, press 1. When you have finished, you may hang up..."

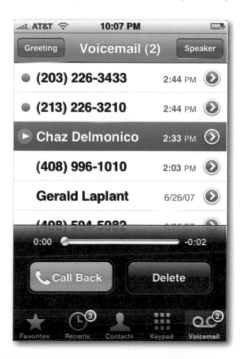

Instead, whenever somebody leaves you a message, the phone wakes up, and a message on the screen lets you know who the message is from. You also hear a sound, unless you've turned that option off (page 245) or turned on the Silence switch (page 12).

That's your cue to tap Home→Phone→Voicemail. There, you see all your messages in a tidy chronological list. (The list shows the callers' names if they're in your Contacts list, or their numbers otherwise.) You can listen to them in any order—you're not forced to listen to your three long-winded friends before discovering that there's an urgent message from your boss. It's a game-changer.

Setup

To access your voicemail, tap Phone on the Home screen, and then tap Voicemail on the Phone screen.

The very first time you visit this screen, the iPhone prompts you to make up a numeric password for your voicemail account—don't worry, you'll never have to enter it again—and to record a "Leave me a message" greeting.

You have two options for the outgoing greeting:

- **Default.** If you're microphone-shy, or if you're someone famous and you don't want stalkers and fans calling just to hear your famous voice, use

this option. It's a prerecorded, somewhat uptight female voice that says, "Your call has been forward to an automatic voice message system. 212-661-7837 is not available." *Beep!*

- **Custom.** This option lets you record your own voice saying, for example, "You've reached my iPhone. You may begin drooling at the tone." Tap Record, hold the iPhone to your head, say your line, and then tap Stop.

  Check how it sounds by tapping Play.

Then just wait for your fans to start leaving you messages!

Using Visual Voicemail

In the voicemail list, a blue dot ● indicates a message that you haven't yet played.

 You can work through your messages even when you're out of AT&T cellular range—on a plane, for example—because the recordings are stored on the iPhone itself.

There are only two tricky things to learn about Visual Voicemail:

- **Tap a message's name twice, not once, to play it.** That's a deviation from the usual iPhone Way, where just *one* tap does the trick. In Visual Voicemail, tapping a message just selects it and activates the Call Back and Delete buttons at the bottom of the screen. You have to tap *twice* to start playback.

- **Turn on Speaker Phone first.** As the name Visual Voicemail suggests, you're *looking* at your voicemail list—which means you're *not* holding the phone up to your head. The first time people try using Visual Voicemail, therefore, they generally hear nothing!

  That's a good argument for hitting the Speaker button *before* tapping messages that you want to play back. That way, you can hear the playback *and* continue looking over the list. (Of course, if privacy is an issue, you can also double-tap a message and then quickly whip the phone up to your ear.)

 If you're listening through the earbuds or a Bluetooth earpiece or car kit, of course, you hear the message playing back through *that*. If you really want to listen through the iPhone's speaker instead, tap Audio, then Speaker Phone. (You switch back the same way.)

Everything else about Visual Voicemail is straightforward. The buttons do exactly what they say:

- **Delete.** The Voicemail list scrolls with a flick of your finger, but you still might want to keep the list manageable by deleting old messages. To do that, tap a message and then tap Delete. The message disappears instantly. (You're not asked to confirm.)

 Tip The iPhone hangs on to old messages for 30 days—even ones you've deleted. To listen to deleted messages that are still on the phone, scroll to the bottom of the list and tap Deleted Messages.

On the Deleted screen, you can Undelete a message that you actually don't want to lose yet (that is, move it back to the Voicemail screen), or tap Clear All to erase these messages for good.

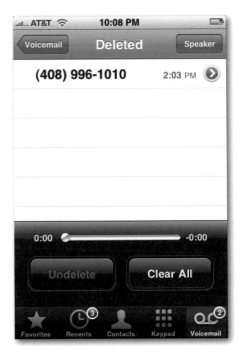

- **Call Back.** Tap a message and then tap Call Back to return the call. Very cool—you never even encounter the person's phone number.

- **Rewind, Fast Forward.** Drag the little white ball in the scroll bar (beneath the list) to skip backward or forward in the message. It's a great way to replay something you didn't catch the first time.

- **Greeting.** Tap this button (upper-left corner) to record your voicemail greeting.

- **Call Details.** Tap the 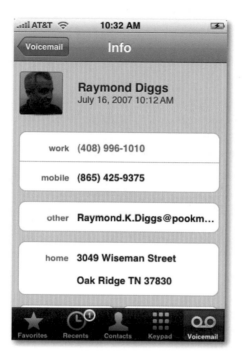 button to open the Info screen for the message that was left for you. Here you'll find out the date and time of the message.

If it was left by somebody who's in your Contacts list, you can see *which* of that person's phone numbers the call came from (indicated in blue type), plus a five-pointed star if that number is in your Favorites list. Oh, and you can add this person to your Favorites list at this point by tapping "Add to Favorites".

If the caller's number isn't in Contacts, you're shown the city and state where that person's phone is registered. And you'll be offered a Create New Contact button and an Add to Existing Contact button, so you can store it for future reference.

In both cases, you also have the option to return the call (right from the Info screen) or fire off a text message.

Dialing in for Messages

As gross and pre-iPhonish though it may sound, you can also dial in for your messages from another phone. (Hey, it could happen.)

To do that, dial your iPhone's number. Wait for the voicemail system to answer.

As your own voicemail greeting plays, dial *, your voicemail password, and then #. You'll hear the Uptight AT&T Lady announce the first "skipped" message (actually the first unplayed message), and then she'll start playing them for you.

After you hear each message, she'll offer you the following options (but you don't have to wait for her to announce them):

- To delete the message, press 7.

- To save it, press 9.

- To replay it, press 4.

- To hear the date, time, and number the message came from, press 5. (You don't hear the lady give you these last two options until you press "zero for more options"—but they work any time you press them.)

 Tip If this whole Visual Voicemail thing freaks you out, you can also dial in for messages the old-fashioned way, right from the iPhone. Open the Keypad (page 34) and hold down the 1 key, just as though it's a speed-dial key on any normal phone.

After a moment, the phone connects to AT&T; you're asked for your password, and then the messages begin to play back, just as described above.

SMS Text Messages

"Texting," as the young whippersnappers call it, was *huge* in Asia and Europe before it began catching on in the United States. These days, however, it's increasingly popular, especially among teenagers and twentysomethings.

SMS stands for Short Messaging Service. An SMS text message is a very short note (under 160 characters—a sentence or two) that you shoot from one cellphone to another. What's so great about it?

- Like a phone call, it's immediate. You get the message off your chest right now.

- As with email, the recipient doesn't have to answer immediately. He can reply at his leisure; the message waits for him even when his phone is turned off.

- Unlike a phone call, it's nondisruptive. You can send someone a text message without worrying that he's in a movie, in class, in a meeting, or anywhere else where talking and holding a phone up to the head would be frowned upon. (And the other person can answer nondisruptively, too, by sending a text message *back*.)

- You have a written record of the exchange. There's no mistaking what the person meant. (Well, at least not because of voice quality. Whether or not you can understand the texting shorthand culture that's evolved from people using no-keyboard cellphones to type English words—"C U 2morrO," and so on—is another matter entirely.)

All AT&T iPhone accounts include 200 free text messages per month (although you can upgrade your account—meaning pay more—if you send more than that). Keep in mind that you use up one of those 200 each time you send *or receive* a message, so they go quickly.

Receiving a Text Message

When someone sends you an SMS, the iPhone plays a quick marimba riff and displays the name or number of the sender *and* the message, in a translucent

message rectangle. If you're using the iPhone at the time, you can tap Ignore (to keep doing what you're doing) or View (to open the message, as shown below).

Otherwise, if the iPhone was asleep, it wakes up and displays the message right on its Unlock screen. You have to unlock the phone and then open the Text program manually. Tap the very first icon in the upper-left corner of the Home screen.

Tip The Text icon on the Home screen bears a little circled number "badge," letting you know how many new text messages are waiting for you.

Either way, the look of the Text program might surprise you. It resembles iChat, Apple's chat program for Macintosh, in which incoming text messages and your replies are displayed as though they're cartoon speech balloons.

To respond to the message, tap in the text box at the bottom of the screen. The iPhone keyboard appears. Type away (page 12), and then tap Send. Assuming your phone has cellular coverage, the message gets sent off immediately.

And if your buddy replies, then the balloon-chat continues, scrolling up the screen.

The Text List

What's cool is that the iPhone retains all of these exchanges. You can review them or resume them at any time by tapping Text on the Home screen. A list of text message conversations appears; a blue dot indicates conversations that contain new messages.

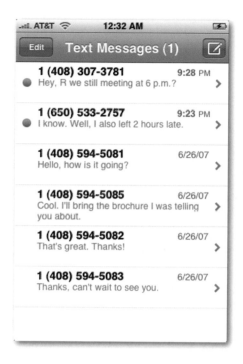

The truth is, these listings represent *people,* not conversations. For example, if you had a text message exchange with Chris last week, a quick way to send a new text message (on a totally different subject) to Chris is to open that "conversation" and simply send a "reply." The iPhone saves you the administrative work of creating a new message, choosing a recipient, and so on.

If having these old exchanges hanging around presents a security (or marital) risk, you can delete it in either of two ways:

- **From the Text Messages list**: The long way: Tap Edit; tap the ⊖ button; finally, tap Delete to confirm.

  The short way: *Swipe* away the conversation. Instead of tapping Edit, just swipe your finger horizontally across the conversation's name (either direction). That makes the Delete confirmation button appear immediately.

- **From within a conversation's speech-balloons screen**: Tap Clear; tap Clear Conversation to confirm.

Sending a New Message

If you want to text somebody with whom you've texted before, the quickest way, as noted above, is simply to resume one of the "conversations" that are already listed in the Text Messages list.

Options to fire off a text message are lurking all over the iPhone. A few examples:

- **In the Contacts, Recents, or Favorites lists.** Tap a person's name in Contacts, or ❯ next to a listing in Recents or Favorites, to open the Info screen; tap Text Message. In other words, sending a text message to anyone whose cellphone number lives in your iPhone is only two taps away.

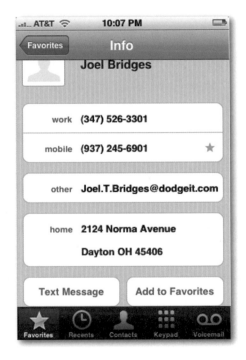

- **In the Text program.** Press the Home→Text icon. The iPhone opens the complete list of messages that you've received. Tap the ✉ button at the top-right corner of the screen to open a new text message window, with the keyboard ready to go.

Address it by tapping the + button, which opens your Contacts list. Tap the person you want to text.

 Note Your *entire* Contacts list appears here, even ones with no cellphone numbers. But you can't text somebody who doesn't have a cellphone number.

In any case, the text message composition screen appears. You're ready to type and send!

 Tip Links that people send you in text messages actually work. For example, if someone sends you a Web address, tap it with your finger to open it in Safari. If someone sends a street address, tap it to open it in Google Maps. And if someone sends a phone number, tap it to dial.

Free Text Messaging

If you think you can keep yourself under the 200-message-per-month limit of most iPhone calling plans (remember, that's sent *and* received), great! You're all set.

 Tip Then again, how are you supposed to know how many text messages you've sent and received so far this month? Your iPhone sure doesn't keep track.

The only way find out is to sign in to *www.wireless.att.com* and click My Account. (The first time you do, you'll have to register by supplying your email address and a Web password.) The Web site offers detailed information about how many minutes you've used so far this month—and how many text messages. Might be worth bookmarking that link in your iPhone's browser.

But if you risk going over that limit, you'll be glad to know there's a way to send all your outgoing text messages to be free.

Enter Teleflip, a free service that converts *email* into *text messages.* Teleflip requires no signup, fee, contract, or personal information whatsoever.

Until recently, the chief use for this service was firing off text messages from your computer to somebody's cellphone.

But the dawn of the iPhone opens up a whole new world for Teleflip. It lets you send an email (which is free with your iPhone plan) that gets received as a text message on the other end. You pay nothing.

To make this happen, create a new email address for each person you might like to text. The email address will look like *2125551212@teleflip.com* (of course, substitute the real phone number for 2125551212). That's it! Any messages you send to that address are free to send, because they're email—but they arrive as text messages!

Chat Programs

No, your eyes do not deceive you. That heading really says "Chat Programs."

Of course, the iPhone itself doesn't *have* any chat programs, like AIM (AOL Instant Messenger), Yahoo Messenger, or MSN Messenger. But that doesn't mean you have to remain chatless.

Thanks to Web sites like Meebo.com, Jivetalk.com, Beejive.com, and FlashIM. com, all of which are accessible from the Web browser on your iPhone, you can chat away with your buddies just as though you're at home on a computer. (Well, on a computer with a touchscreen keyboard two inches wide.)

Call Waiting

Call Waiting has been around for years. With a call waiting feature, when you're on one phone call, you hear a beep in your ear indicating someone else is calling in. You can tap the Flash key on your phone—if you know which one it is—to answer the second call while you put the first one on hold.

Some people don't use Call Waiting because it's rude to both callers. Others don't use it because they have no idea what the Flash key is.

On the iPhone, when a second call comes in, the phone rings (and/or vibrates) as usual, and the screen displays the name or number of the caller, just as it always does. Buttons on the screen offer you three choices:

- **Ignore.** The incoming call goes straight to voicemail. Your first caller has no idea that anything's happened.

- **Hold Call + Answer.** This button gives you the traditional Call Waiting effect. You say, "Can you hold on a sec? I've got another call" to the first caller. The iPhone puts her on hold, and you connect to the second caller.

  At this point, you can jump back and forth between the two calls, or you can merge them into a conference call, just as described on page 36.

- **End Call + Answer.** Tapping this button hangs up on the first call and takes the second one.

If Call Waiting seems a bit disruptive all the way around, you can turn it off; see page 256. When Call Waiting is turned off, incoming calls go straight to voicemail when you're on the phone.

Caller ID

Caller ID is another classic cellphone feature. It's the one that displays the phone number of the incoming call (and sometimes the name of the caller).

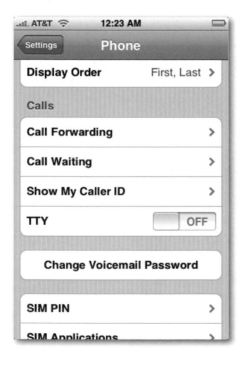

The only thing worth noting about the iPhone's own implementation of Caller ID is that you can prevent *your* number from appearing when you call *other* people's phones.

From the Home screen, tap Settings→Phone→Show MyCaller ID, and then tap the On/Off switch.

Call Forwarding

Here's a pretty cool feature you may not even have known you had. It lets you route all calls made to your iPhone number to a *different* number. How is this useful? Let us count the ways:

- When you're home. You can have your cellphone's calls ring your home number, so you can use any extension in the house, and so you don't miss any calls while the iPhone is turned off or charging.

- When you send your iPhone to Apple for battery replacement (page 277), you can forward the calls you would have missed to your home or work phone number.

- When you're overseas, you can forward the number to one of the Web-based services that answers your voicemail and sends it to you as an email attachment (like GrandCentral.com or CallWave.com).

- When you're going to be in a place with little or no AT&T cell coverage (Alaska, say), you can have your calls forwarded to your hotel or a friend's cellphone.

You have to turn on Call Forwarding while you're still in an area with AT&T coverage. Start at the Home screen. Tap Settings→ Phone→Call Forwarding, turn Call Forwarding on, and then tap in the new phone number. That's all there is to it —your iPhone will no longer ring.

At least not until you turn the same switch off again.

Bluetooth Earpieces and Car Kits

The iPhone has more antennas than an ant colony: one for the cellular network, one for Wi-Fi hot spots, and a third for Bluetooth.

Bluetooth is a short-range wireless *cable elimination* technology. It's designed to untether you from equipment that would ordinarily require a cord. Bluetooth crops up in computers (print from a laptop to a Bluetooth printer), in game consoles (like Sony's wireless PlayStation controller), and above all, in cellphones.

There are all kinds of things Bluetooth *can* do in cellphones, like transmitting cameraphone photos to computers, wirelessly syncing your address book from a computer, or letting the phone in your pocket serve as a wireless Internet antenna for your laptop. But the iPhone can do only one Bluetooth thing: hands-free calling.

To be precise, it works with those tiny wireless Bluetooth earpieces, of the sort you see clipped to tech-savvy people's ears in public, as well as with cars with built-in Bluetooth phone systems. If your car has one of these "car kits" (Acura, Prius, and many other models include them), you hear the other person's voice through your stereo speakers, and there's a microphone built into your steering wheel or rear-view mirror. You keep your hands on the wheel the whole time.

Pairing with a Bluetooth Earpiece

So far, Bluetooth hands-free systems have been embraced primarily by the world's geeks for one simple reason: It's *way* too complicated to pair the earpiece (or car) with the phone.

So what's pairing? That's the system of "marrying" a phone to a Bluetooth earpiece, so that each works only with the other. If you didn't do this pairing, then some other guy passing on the sidewalk might hear your conversation through *his* earpiece. And you probably wouldn't like that.

The pairing process is different for every cellphone and every Bluetooth earpiece. Usually it involves a sequence like this:

❶ **On the earpiece, turn on Bluetooth. Make the earpiece discoverable.** *Discoverable* just means that your phone can "see" it. You'll have to consult the earpiece's instructions to learn how to do so.

❷ **On the iPhone, tap Home→Settings→General→Bluetooth. Turn Bluetooth to On.** The iPhone immediately begins searching for nearby

Bluetooth equipment. If all goes well, you'll see the name of your earpiece show up on the screen.

❸ **Tap the earpiece's name. Type in the passcode.** The *passcode* is a number, usually four or six digits, that must be typed into the phone within about a minute. You have to enter this only once, during the initial pairing process. The idea is to prevent some evildoer sitting nearby in the airport waiting lounge, for example, to secretly pair *his* earpiece with *your* iPhone.

The user manual for your earpiece should tell you what the passcode is.

When you're using a Bluetooth earpiece, you *dial* using the iPhone itself. You generally use the iPhone's own volume controls, too. You generally press a button on the earpiece itself to answer an incoming call, to swap Call Waiting calls, and to end a call.

If you're having any problems making a particular earpiece work, Google it. Type "iPhone Motorola H800 earpiece," for example. Chances are good that you'll find a writeup by somebody who's worked through the setup and made it work.

Apple's Bluetooth Earpiece

Apple's own Bluetooth earpiece ($130), sold just for the iPhone, is one of the tiniest and simplest earpieces on the market. It has several advantages over other companies' earpieces. For example, it comes with a charging cradle that looks and works just like the iPhone's, but has a hole for charging the earpiece simultaneously.

Better yet, this earpiece pairs itself with your phone *automatically.* You don't have to go through any of that multi-step riga-marole. All you have to do is put the iPhone and the headset into the charging cradle simultaneously—and the deed is done.

There's only one button on the earpiece. Press it to connect it to the iPhone. When the iPhone is connected, you'll see a blue or white ✳ icon appear at the top of the iPhone's screen (depending on the background color of the program you're using).

> **Note** When Bluetooth is turned on but the earpiece isn't, or when the earpiece isn't nearby, the ✳ icon appears in gray.

To use this earpiece, pop it into your ear. To make a call or adjust the volume, you use the phone itself as usual. The only difference is that you hear the audio in your ear. The microphone is the little stub that points toward your chin (the iPhone's own mike is turned off).

You answer a call by pressing the earpiece button; you hang up by pressing it again.

Car Kits

The iPhone works beautifully with Bluetooth car kits, too. The pairing procedure generally goes exactly as described above: You make the car discoverable, enter the passcode on the iPhone, and then make the connection.

Once you're paired up, you can answer an incoming call by pressing a button on your steering wheel, for example. You make calls either from the iPhone or, in some cars, by dialing the number on the car's own touch screen.

Of course, studies show that it's the act of driving while conversing that causes accidents—not actually holding the phone. So the hands-free system is less for safety than for convenience and compliance with state laws.

4 | Music and Video

O f the iPhone's Big Three talents—phone, Internet, and iPod—its iPoddishness may be the most successful. This function, after all, is the only one that doesn't require the participation of AT&T and its network. It works even on planes and in subways. And it's the iPhone function that gets the most impressive battery life (almost 24 hours of music playback).

This chapter assumes that you've already loaded some music or video onto your iPhone, as described in Chapter 11.

To enter iPod Land, press the Home button, and then tap the orange iPod icon at the lower-right corner of the screen.

List Land

The iPod program begins with lists—lots of lists. The first four icons at the bottom of the screen represent your starter lists, as follows:

- **Playlists.** A *playlist* is a group of songs that you've placed together, in a sequence that makes sense to you. One might consist of party tunes; another might hold romantic dinnertime music; a third might be drum-heavy workout cuts.

  You create playlists in the iTunes software, as described on page 202. After you sync the iPhone with your computer, those playlists appear here.

  Scroll the list by dragging your finger or by flicking. To see what songs or videos are in a playlist, tap its name. (The > symbol in an iPod menu always means, "Tap to see what's in this list.")

 Tip Here's a universal iPhone convention: Anywhere you're asked to *drill down* from one list to another—from a playlist to the songs inside, for example—you can backtrack by tapping the blue button at the upper-left corner of the screen. Its name changes to tell you what screen you came from (Playlists, for example).

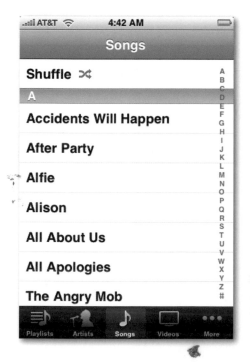

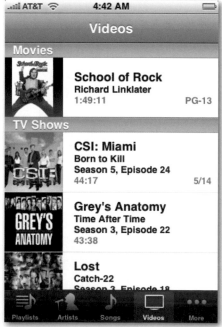

To start playing a song or video once you see it in the playlist list, tap it.

 For details on the On-the-Go Playlist, which is the first item in Playlists, see page 86.

- **Artists.** This list identifies all of the bands, orchestras, or singers in your collection. Even if you have only one song from a certain performer, it shows up here.

  Once again, you drill down to the list of individual songs or videos by tapping an artist's name. At that point, tap any song or video to begin playing it.

- **Songs.** Here's an alphabetical list of every song on your iPhone. Scroll or flick through it, or use the index at the right side of the screen to jump to a letter of the alphabet. (It works exactly as described on page 31.) Tap anything to begin playing it.

- **Videos.** Tap this icon for one-stop browsing of all the video material on your phone, organized by category: Movies, TV Shows, Music Videos, and Podcasts—video podcasts, that is. (You see only one listing for each pod-caster, along with the number of episodes you've got). A handy thumb-nail photo next to each video gives you a hint as to what's in it, and you also see the total playing time of each one.

  You can probably guess, at this point, how you start one playing: by tap-ping its name. But don't forget to rotate the iPhone 90 degrees; all videos play in landscape orientation (the wide way).

 At the bottom of any of these lists, you'll see the total number of items *in* that list: "76 Songs," for example. At the top of the screen, you may see the Now Playing button, which opens up the playback screen (page 77) of whatever's playing.

Other Lists

Those four lists—Playlists, Artists, Songs, Videos—are only suggestions. On a *real* iPod, of course, you can slice and dice your music collection in all kinds of other listy ways: by Album, Genre, Composer, and so on.

You can do that on the iPhone, too; there just isn't room across the bottom row to hold more than four list icons at a time.

To view some of the most useful secondary lists, tap the fifth and final icon, labeled More. The More screen appears, listing a bunch of other ways to view your collection:

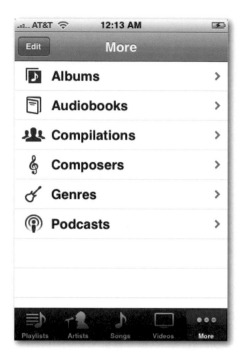

- **Albums.** That's right, it's a list of all the CDs from which your music collection is derived, complete with miniature pictures of the album art. Tap an album's name to see a list of songs that came from it; tap a song to start playing it.

- **Audiobooks.** One of the great pricey joys of life is listening to digital "books on tape" that you've bought from Audible.com (see page 201). They show up in this list. (Audio books you've ripped from CDs don't show up here—only ones you've downloaded from Audible.)

Tip In a hurry? You can speed up the playback without making the narrator sound like a chipmunk—or slow the narrator down if he's talking too fast. Page 259 has the details.

- **Compilations.** A *compilation* is one of those albums that's been put together from many different performers. You know: "Zither Hits of the 1600s," "Kazoo Classics," and so on. You're supposed to turn on the Compilation checkbox manually, in iTunes, to identify songs that belong together in this way. Once you've done that, all songs that belong to compilations you've created show up in this list.

- **Composers.** Here's your whole music collection sorted by composer—a crumb that the iPod/iPhone creators have thrown to classical-music fans.

- **Genres.** Tap this item to sort your collection by musical genre (that is, style): Pop, Rock, World, Podcast, Gospel, or whatever.

- **Podcasts.** Here are all your podcasts (page 200), listed by creator. A blue dot indicates that you haven't yet listened to some of the podcasts by a certain podcaster. Similarly, if you tap a podcast's name to drill down, you'll see the individual episodes, once again marked by blue "you haven't heard me yet" dots.

Customizing List Land

Now you know how to sort your collection by every conceivable criterion. But what if you're a huge podcast nut? Are you really expected to open up the More screen (shown on the facing page) every time you want to see your list of podcasts? Or what if you frequently want access to your audiobooks or composer list?

Fortunately, you can add the icons of these lists to the bottom of the main iPod screen, where the four starter categories now appear (Playlists, Artists, Songs, Videos). That is, you can replace or rearrange the icons that show up here, so that the lists you use most frequently are easier to open.

To renovate the four starter icons, tap the More button and then tap the Edit button (upper-left corner). You arrive at the Configure screen.

Here's the complete list of music-and-video sorting lists: Albums, Podcasts, Audiobooks, Genres, Composers, Compilations, Playlists, Artists, Songs, and Videos.

To replace one of the four starter icons at the bottom, use a finger to drag an icon from the top half of the screen downward, directly onto the *existing* icon you want to replace. It lights up to show the success of your drag.

When you release your finger, you'll see that the new icon has replaced the old one. Tap Done in the upper-right corner.

Oh, and while you're on the Edit screen: You can also take this opportunity to **rearrange** the first four icons at the bottom. Drag them around with your finger. It's fun for the whole family.

Cover Flow

Anytime you're using the iPhone's iPod personality, whether you're playing music or just flipping through your lists, you can rotate the iPhone 90 degrees in either direction—so it's in landscape orientation—to turn on Cover Flow. *Nothing* gets oohs and ahhhs from the admiring crowd like Cover Flow.

In Cover Flow, the screen goes dark for a moment—and then it reappears, showing two-inch-tall album covers, floating on a black background. Push or flick with your fingers to make them fly and flip over in 3-D space, as though they're CDs in a record-store rack.

If you tap one (or tap the little ❶ button in the lower-right corner), the album flips around so you can see the "back" of it, containing a list of songs from that album. Tap a song to start playing it; tap the ‖ in the lower-left corner to pause. Tap the back (or the ❶ button) again to flip the album cover back to the front and continue browsing.

To turn off Cover Flow, rotate the iPhone upright again.

So what, exactly, is Cover Flow for? You could argue that it's a unique way to browse your collection, to seek inspiration in your collection without having to stare at scrolling lists of text.

But you could also argue that it's just Apple's engineers showing off.

The Now Playing Screen (Music)

Whenever a song is playing, the Now Playing screen appears, filled with information and controls for your playback pleasure.

For example:

- **Return arrow.** At the top-left corner of the screen, the fat, left-pointing arrow means, "Return to the list whence this song came." It takes you back to the list of songs in this album, playlist, or whatever.

- **Song info.** Center top: the artist name, track name, and album name. Nothing to tap here, folks. Move along.

- **Album list.** At the top-*right* corner, you see a three-line icon that seems to say, "list." Tap it to view a list of all songs on *this* song's album.

 You can double-tap the big album art picture to open the track list, too. It's a bigger target.

This screen offers three enjoyable activities. You can jump directly to another cut by tapping its name. You can check out the durations of the songs in this album.

And you can *rate* a song, ranking it from one to five stars, by tapping its name and then tapping one of the five dots at the top of the screen. If you tap dot number 3, for example, then the first three dots all turn into stars. You've just given that song three stars. When you next sync your iPhone with your computer, the ratings you've applied magically show up on the same songs in iTunes.

To return to the Now Playing screen, tap the upper-right icon once again. (Once you tap, that icon looks like the album cover.) Or, for a bigger target, double-tap any blank part of the screen.

Return to list

Songs on this album

Swipe to return to the list

Volume slider

- **Album art.** Most of the screen is filled with a bright, colorful shot of the original CD's album art. (If none is available—if you're listening to a song *you* wrote, for example—you see a big gray generic musical-note picture.)

Controlling Playback (Music)

Once you're on the Now Playing screen, a few controls await your fingertip—some obvious and some not so obvious.

- **Play/Pause (▶/II) button.** The Pause button looks like this **II** when the music is playing. If you do pause the music, the button turns into the Play button (▶).

 If you're wearing the earbuds, pinching the microphone clicker serves the same purpose: It's a Play/Pause control.

Incidentally, when you plug in headphones, the iPhone's built-in speaker turns off, but when you unplug the headphones, your music pauses instead of switching abruptly back to the speaker. You may have to unlock the iPhone and navigate to the iPod program to resume playback.

- **Previous, Next (I◀◀, ▶▶I).** These buttons work exactly as they do on an iPod. That is, tap **I◀◀** to skip to the beginning of this song (or, if you're already at the beginning, to the previous song). Tap **▶▶I** to skip to the next song.

 If you're wearing the earbuds, you can pinch the clicker *twice* to skip to the next song.

If you hold down one of these buttons instead of tapping, you rewind or fast-forward. It's rather cool, actually—you get to hear the music speeding by as you keep your finger down, without turning the singer into a chipmunk. The rewinding or fast-forwarding accelerates if you keep holding down the button.

- **Volume.** You can drag the round, white handle of this scroll bar (bottom of the screen) to adjust the volume—or you can use the volume keys on the left side of the phone.

Of course, you probably didn't need a handsome full-color book to tell you what those basic playback controls are for. But there's also a trio of *secret* controls that don't appear until you tap anywhere on an empty part of the screen (for example, on the album cover):

- **Loop button.** If you *really* love a certain album or playlist, you can command the iPhone to play it over and over again, beginning to end. Just tap the Loop button (⟳) so it turns blue (⟳).

 Tap the Loop button a second time to endlessly loop *just this song.*

A tiny clock icon appears on the blue loop graphic, like this ⟳, to let you know that you've entered this mode. Tap a third time to turn off looping.

Hidden controls

- **Scroll slider.** This slider (top of the screen) reveals three useful statistics: how much of the song you've heard, in minutes:seconds format (at the left end), how much time remains (at the right end), and which slot this song occupies in the current playlist or album.

  To operate the slider, drag the tiny round handle with your finger. (Just tapping directly on the spot you want to hear doesn't work.)

- **Shuffle button.** Ordinarily, the iPhone plays the songs in an album sequentially, from beginning to end. But if you love surprises, tap the ✗ button so it turns blue. Now you'll hear the songs on the album in random order.

To hide the slider, Loop, and Shuffle buttons, tap an empty part of the screen once again.

By the way, there's nothing to stop you from turning on **both** Shuffle **and** Loop, meaning that you'll hear the songs on the album played endlessly, but never in the same order twice.

 Note Did you ever notice the tiny grille (pinholes) at the bottom inside of the iPhone's charging cradle? They're there to let the sound out. That's right: you can use the iPhone as a desktop music machine, even while it's charging. The holes actually help matters, because the sound bounces off the desktop instead of shooting out into space away from you. (You can't listen while you sync, alas.)

Multi(music)tasking

Once you're playing music, it keeps right on playing, even if you press the Home button and move on to do some other work on the iPhone. After all, the only thing more pleasurable than surfing the Web is surfing it to a Beach Boys soundtrack.

Music is playing

A tiny ▶ icon at the top of the screen reminds you that music is still playing. That's handy if the earbuds are plugged in but you're not wearing them.

Or, if you've got something else to do—like jogging, driving, or performing surgery—tap the Sleep/Wake switch to turn off the screen. The music will keep playing, but you'll save battery power.

 Tip Even with the screen off, you can still adjust the music volume (use the keys on the left side of the phone), pause the music (pinch the earbud clicker once), or advance to the next song (pinch it twice).

If a phone call comes in, the music fades, and you hear your chosen ring-tone—through your earbuds, if you're wearing them. Squeeze the clicker on the earbud cord, or tap the Sleep/Wake switch, to answer the call. When the call ends, the music fades back in, right where it had stopped.

Controlling Playback (Video)

Having a bunch of sliders and buttons on the screen doesn't inconvenience you much when you're listening to music. The action is in your ears, not on the screen.

But when you're playing video, *anything* else on the screen is distracting, so Apple hides the video playback controls. Tap the screen once to make them appear, and again to make them disappear.

Here's what they do:

- **Done.** Tap this blue button, in the top-left corner, to stop playback and return to the master list of videos.

- **Scroll slider.** This progress indicator (top of the screen) is exactly like the one you see when you're playing music. You see the elapsed time, remaining time, and a little white round handle that you can drag to jump forward or back in the video.

- **Zoom/Unzoom.** In the top-right corner, a little ⬈ or ⬊ button appears. Tap it to adjust the zoom level of the video, as described on the facing page.

- **Play/Pause (▶/II).** These buttons (and the earbud clicker) do the same thing to video as they do to music: alternate between playing and pausing.

- **Previous, Next (I◀◀, ▶▶I).** Hold down your finger to rewind or fast-forward the video. The longer you hold, the faster the zipping. (When you fast-forward, you even get to hear the sped-up audio, at least for the first few seconds.)

    If you're watching a movie from the iTunes Music Store, you may be surprised to discover that it comes with predefined chapter markers, just like a DVD. Internally, it's divided up into scenes. You can tap the I◀◀ or ▶▶I button to skip to the previous or next chapter marker—a great way to navigate a long movie quickly.

 Tip If you're wearing the earbuds, you can pinch the clicker *twice* to skip to the next chapter.

- **Volume.** You can drag the round, white handle of this scroll bar (bottom of the screen) to adjust the volume—or you can use the volume keys on the left side of the phone.

When you reach the end of a video, the iPhone asks if you want to keep it or delete it. It's a thoughtful gesture, considering that videos occupy an enormous chunk of the iPhone's memory. (Deleting it from the iPhone doesn't delete it from your computer.)

 Tip Playing a video to the end isn't the only way to delete it. On the Videos list (page 73), you can swipe your finger across a video's name; tap Delete to confirm.

Zoom/Unzoom

The iPhone's screen is bright, vibrant, and stunningly sharp. (It's got 320 by 480 pixels, crammed so tightly that there are 160 of them per inch, which is nearly twice the resolution of a computer screen.)

It's not, however, the right shape for videos.

Standard TV shows are squarish, not rectangular. So when you watch TV shows, you get black letterbox columns on either side of the picture.

Movies have the opposite problem. They're *too* wide for the iPhone screen. So when you watch movies, you wind up with *horizontal* letterbox bars above and below the picture.

Some people are fine with that. After all, HDTV sets have the same problem; people are used to it. At least when letterbox bars are onscreen, you know you're seeing the complete composition of the scene the director intended.

Other people can't stand letterbox bars. You're already watching on a pretty small screen; why sacrifice some of that precious area to black bars?

Fortunately, the iPhone gives you a choice. If you double-tap the video as it plays, you zoom in, magnifying the image so it fills the entire screen. Or, if the playback controls are visible, you can also tap ⬊ or ⬋.

Truth is, part of the image is now off the screen; now you're not seeing the entire composition as originally created. You lose the top and bottom of TV scenes, or the left and right edges of movie scenes.

Fortunately, if this effect winds up chopping off something important—some text on the screen, for example—restoring the original letterbox view is just another double-tap away.

Familiar iPod Features

In certain respects, the iPhone is *not* an iPod. It doesn't have a click wheel, it doesn't come with any games, it doesn't display lyrics, it can't output video to a TV set, and it doesn't offer disk mode (where the iPod acts as a hard drive for transporting computer files). At least not in version 1.

 Tip OK, OK—there actually *is* a way to simulate iPod disk mode on the iPhone. Just download iPhone Drive, a shareware program available from this book's "Missing CD" page at *www.missingmanuals.com*.

It does have a long list of traditional iPod features, though. You just have to know where to find them.

Volume Limiter

It's now established fact: Listening to a lot of loud music through earphones can damage your hearing. Pump it today, pay for it tomorrow.

MP3 players can be sinister that way, because in noisy places like planes and city streets, people turn up the volume much louder than they would in a quiet place, and they don't even realize how high they've cranked it. No wonder parents worry about their kids.

That's why Apple created the password-protected volume limiter. It lets parents program their children's iPods (and now iPhones) to max out at a certain volume level that can be surpassed only with the password.

To set up the volume limiter and its password, see page 260.

Sound Check

This feature smooths out the master volume levels of tracks from different albums, helping to compensate for differences in their original recording levels. It doesn't deprive you of peaks and valleys in the music volume, of course—it affects only the baseline level. You turn it on or off in Settings (page 259).

Equalization

Like any good music player these days, the iPhone offers an EQ function: a long list of presets, each of which affects your music differently by boosting or throttling back various frequencies. One might bring out the bass to goose up your hip-hop tunes; another might emphasize the midrange for clearer vocals; and so on. To turn the EQ on or off, or to choose a different preset, see page 259.

On-the-Go Playlist

During the first few years of the iPod Age, you could create playlists only in iTunes. You couldn't create one when you were out and about—to kill time standing in line at the Department of Motor Vehicles, for example, or to whip together a little music flow to impress a hot date.

Now you can.

- **Creating an On-the-Go Playlist.** Open the iPod program (Home→iPod). Tap Playlists. At the top of the Playlists screen, tap On-The-Go.

    Now a master list of all your songs appears. Each time you see one worth adding to your On-the-Go Playlist, tap its name (or the + button). You can also tap one of the icons at the bottom, like Playlists, Artists, or Videos, to find the stuff you want.

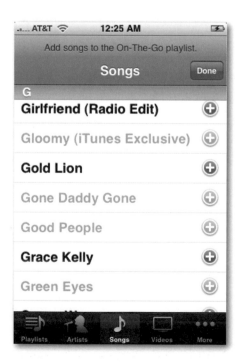

When you're finished, tap Done. Your playlist is ready to play, just as you would any playlist.

- **Editing the On-the-Go Playlist.** On the Playlists screen, tap On-The-Go; on the next screen, tap Edit. Here you're offered a Clear Playlist command, which (after a confirmation request) empties the list completely.

  You also see the universal iPhone Delete symbol (⊖). Tap it, and then tap the Delete confirmation button on the right side, to remove a song from the playlist.

  To add more songs to the list, tap the ✚ button at the top left. You're now shown the list of songs in the *current* playlist; you can tap Playlists to switch to a different playlist, or tap one of the other buttons at the bottom of the screen, like Artists or Songs, to view your music collection in those list formats. Each time you see a song worth adding, tap it.

  Finally, note the "grip strip" at the right edge of the screen (≡). With your finger, drag these handles up or down to rearrange the songs in your OTG playlist. When your editing job is complete, tap Done.

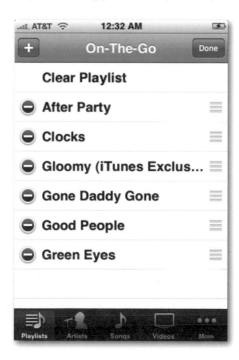

5 | Photos and Camera

This is a short chapter on a short subject: the iPhone's ability to display photos copied over from your computer, and to take new pictures with its built-in camera.

You've probably never seen digital pictures look this good on a pocket gadget. The iPhone screen is bright, the color are vivid, and the super-high pixel density makes every shot of your life look cracklin' sharp.

The built-in 2-megapixel camera takes 1600-by-1200-pixel images. This camera is *capable* of taking photos that look every bit as good as what you'd get from a dedicated camera. Not all of its work looks that good, though: with moving subjects or in low light, it's pretty obvious that you used a cameraphone.

Even so, some camera is better than no camera when life's little photo ops crop up.

Opening Photos

In Chapter 12, you can read about how you choose which photos you want copied to your iPhone.

After the sync is done, you can drill down to a certain set of photos like so:

❶ **On the Home screen, tap Photos.**

The Photo Albums screen appears. First in the list is Camera Roll, which means, "Pictures you've taken with the iPhone."

Next is Photo Library, which means *all* of the photos you've selected to copy from your Mac or PC.

After that is the list of *albums* you brought over from the computer. (An album is the photo equivalent of a playlist. It's a subset of photos, in a sequence you've selected.)

❷ **Tap one of the rolls or albums.**

Now the screen fills with 20 postage stamp-sized thumbnails of the photos in this roll or album. You can scroll this list by flicking.

❸ **Tap the photo you want to see.**

It fills the screen, in all its glory.

Flicking, Rotating, Zooming, and Panning

Once a photo is open at full size, you have your chance to perform the four most famous and most dazzling tricks of the iPhone: flicking, rotating, zooming, and panning a photo.

- **Flicking** (page 17) is how you advance to the next picture in the batch. Flick from right to left. (Flick from left to right to view the *previous* photo.)

- **Rotating** is what you do when a horizontal photo appears on the upright iPhone, which makes the photo look small and fills most of the screen with blackness.

  Just turn the iPhone 90 degrees in either direction. Like magic, the photo itself rotates and enlarges to fill its new, wider canvas. No taps required. (This doesn't work when the phone is flat on its back—on a table, for example. It has to be more or less upright.)

  This trick also works the other way—that is, you can also make a *vertical* photo fit better when you're holding the iPhone horizontally. Just rotate the iPhone back upright.

 Tip When the iPhone is rotated, all of the controls and gestures reorient themselves. For example, flicking right to left still brings on the next photo, even if you're now holding the iPhone the wide way.

- **Zooming** a photo means magnifying it, and it's a blast. One quick way is to double-tap the photo; the iPhone zooms in on the portion you tapped, doubling its size.

  Another way is to use the two-finger spread technique (page 18), which gives you more control over what gets magnified and by how much. (Remember, the iPhone doesn't actually store the giganto ten-mega-

pixel originals of pictures you took with your fancy digital camera—only scaled-down, iPhone-appropriate versions—so you can't zoom in more than about three times the original size.)

Once you've spread a photo bigger, you can then pinch the screen to scale it down again. Or just double-tap a zoomed photo to restore its original size. (You can't flick over to the next photo until you've restored the first one to original size.)

- **Panning** means moving a photo around on the screen after you've zoomed in. Just drag your finger to do that; no scroll bars are necessary.

Deleting Photos

If some photo no longer meets your exacting standards, you can delete it. But this action is trickier than you may think.

- **If you took the picture using the iPhone,** no sweat. Open the photo and then tap the 🗑 button. When you tap Delete Photo to confirm, that picture's gone.

- **If the photo was synced to the iPhone from your computer,** well, that's life. The iPhone remains a *mirror* of what's on the computer. In other words, you can't delete the photo right on the phone. Delete it from the original album on your computer (which does *not* mean deleting it from the computer altogether). The next time you sync the iPhone, the photo disappears from it, too.

Photo Controls

If you tap the screen once, some useful controls appear. They remain on the screen for only a couple of seconds, so as not to ruin the majesty of your photo, so act now.

- **Album name.** You can return to the thumbnails page by tapping the screen once, which summons the playback controls, and then tapping the album name in the upper-left corner.

- **Photo number.** The top of the screen says, "88 of 405," for example, meaning that this is the 88th photo out of 405 in the set.

- **Send icon.** Tap the icon in the lower left if you want to do something more with this photo than just staring at it. You can use it as your iPhone's wallpaper, send it by email, or use it as somebody's headshot in your Contacts list. All three of these techniques are described in the next section.

- **Previous/Next arrows.** These white arrows are provided for the benefit of people who haven't quite figured out that they can *flick* to summon the previous or next photo.

- **Slideshow (▶) button.** Flicking is fun. But starting an automatic slide-show has charms all its own. Its gives other people a better view of the pictures, for one thing, since your hand stays out of their way. It also lets you use some very cool *transition* effects—crossfades, wipes, and Apple's classic rotating-cube effect, for example.

  Just tap the ▶ button to begin the slideshow of the current album or roll, starting with the photo that's already on the screen. You can specify how many seconds each photo hangs around, and what kind of visual transition effect you want between them, by tapping Home→Settings→ Photos (page 260). You can even turn on looping or random shuffling of photos there, too.

  While the slideshow is going on, avoid touching the screen—that stops the show. But feel free to turn the iPhone 90 degrees to accommodate landscape-orientation photos as they come up; the slideshow keeps right on going.

 Tip What kind of slideshow would it be without background music? Tap Home→iPod, and start a song playing. Yank out the earbuds, so that the music comes out of the speaker instead.

Now hit Home→Photos and start the slideshow—with music!

Photo Wallpaper

Wallpaper, in the world of iPhone, refers to the photo that appears on the Unlock screen every time you wake the iPhone. On a new iPhone, an Earth-from-space photo appears there.

You can replace the Earth very easily (at least the photo of it), either with one of your photos or one of Apple's.

Use One of Your Photos

Open one of your photos, as described in the previous pages. Tap the 📤 button, and then tap Use as Wallpaper.

You're now offered the Move and Scale screen so you can fit your rectangular photo within the square wallpaper "frame." Pinch or spread to enlarge the shot (page 18); drag your finger on the screen to scroll and center it.

Finally, tap Set Wallpaper to commit the photo to your Unlock screen.

Use an Apple Photo

The iPhone comes stocked with a few professional, presized photos that you can use as your Unlock-screen wallpaper until you get your own photographic skills in shape.

To find them, start on the Home screen. Tap Settings→Wallpaper→Wallpaper. You see a screen full of thumbnail miniatures; tap one to see what it looks like at full size. If it looks good, tap Set Wallpaper. (How did Apple get the rights to the Mona Lisa, anyway?)

Photos by Email—and by Text Message

You can send any photo—one you've taken with the iPhone, or one you've transferred from your computer—by email, which comes in handy more often than you might think. It's useful when you're out shopping and want to seek your spouse's opinion on something you're about to buy. It's great when you want to give your buddies a glimpse of whatever hell or heaven you're experiencing at the moment.

Once you're in the Photos program, tap the 📤 button, and then tap Email Photo. Now you can email it to someone, right from the phone. The iPhone automatically scales, rotates, and attaches the photo to a new outgoing message. All you have to do is address it (page 150) and hit Send. (The fine print: You can attach only one photo per email. Photo resolution is reduced to 640 x 480 pixels. Void where prohibited.)

Sending Photos to Cellphones

Now, if you had an ordinary cellphone, you'd be able to do something that's quick and useful—send a photo as a ***text message.*** It winds up on the screen of the other guy's cellphone.

That's a delicious feature, almost handier than sending a photo by email. After all, your friends and relatives don't sit in front of their computers all day and all night (unless they're serious geeks).

Alas, the iPhone is one of the very few phones that can't send or receive MMS messages (multimedia messaging service), the technology required for this trick. Officially speaking, you can send photos only as ***email*** attachments. And very few cellphones can receive email, let alone with attachments.

Ah, but this is why you bought an iPhone book—for cool workarounds like this one.

It turns out that there *is* a way to send email, with photo attachments, to almost any cellphone. You just have to know the secret address to use—which is determined by the cellphone carrier your recipient uses.

In each of the following examples, suppose that (212) 555-1212 is the other guy's cellphone number. Here's how to address your outgoing photo email to make sure he gets it.

- **Alltel.** 2125551212@message.alltel.com
- **AT&T.** 2125551212@mms.att.net
- **Sprint.** 2125551212@messaging.sprintpcs.com
- **T-Mobile.** 2125551212@tmomail.net
- **US Cellular.** 2125551212@mms.uscc.net
- **Verizon Wireless.** 2125551212@vzwpix.com
- **Virgin Mobile.** 2125551212@vmobl.com

So how will you ever remember these? You won't. Just record the proper address as a secondary email address in the Contacts program for each person who might enjoy your photos.

Then, when you want to send a photo, proceed as described on page 97—but tap this special email address, and send away! The recipient receives a regular picture text message—yes, an MMS message—even though the iPhone doesn't do MMS!

Headshots for Contacts

If you're viewing a photo of somebody who's listed in Contacts, you can use it (or part of it) as her headshot. After that, her photo appears on your screen every time she calls.

Open a photo. Tap the ⬀ button, and then tap Assign To Contact.

Now your address book list pops up, so that you can assign the selected photo to the person it's a photo of.

If you tap a name, you're then shown a preview of what the photo will look like when that person calls. Welcome to the Move and Scale screen. It works just as it does when you set wallpaper, as described earlier. But when choosing a headshot for a contact, it's even more important. You'll want to crop the photo and shift it in the frame, so that only *that person* is visible. It's a great way to isolate one person in a group shot, for example.

Start by enlarging the photo: Spread your thumb and forefinger against the glass. As you go, *shift* the photo's placement in the frame with a one-finger drag. When you've got the person correctly enlarged and centered, tap Set Photo.

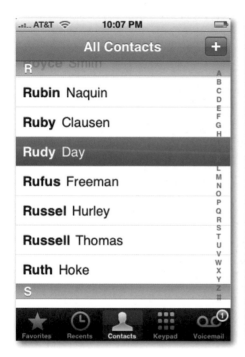

The Camera

The iPhone's camera is the little hole on the back, in the upper-left corner, and the best term for it may be "no frills." There's no flash, no zoom, no image adjustments of any kind. In short, it's just like the camera on most cameraphones.

There's no way to frame up a self-portrait. (And no, the chrome Apple logo on the back is *not* a self-portrait mirror. Unless all you care about is how your nostril looks.)

All the same, the camera is capable of surprisingly clear, sharp, vivid photos (1600 x 1200 pixels)—as long as your subject is sitting still and well lit. Action shots come out blurry, and dim-light shots come out rather grainy.

All right—now that you know what you're in for, here's how it works.

On the Home screen, tap Camera. During the two seconds that it takes the Camera program to warm up, you see a very cool shutter iris-opening effect.

Now frame up the shot, using the iPhone screen as your viewfinder. (At 3.5 inches, it's most likely the largest digital-camera viewfinder you've ever used.) You can turn it 90 degrees for a wider shot, if you like.

When the composition looks good, tap the (○) button. You hear the *snap!* sound of a picture successfully taken.

You get to admire your work for only about half a second—and then the photo slurps itself into the 🗇 icon at the lower-left corner of the screen. That's Apple's subtle way of saying, "Tap here to see the pictures you've taken!" In the meantime, the camera's first priority is getting ready to take another shot.

Reviewing Your Photos

If you do want a look at the pictures you've taken, you have two choices:

- **Tap the 🗂 icon at the lower-left corner of the Camera screen.** You open the screen full of thumbnails of pictures you've taken with the iPhone.

- **From the Home screen, tap Photos→Camera Roll.** "Camera Roll" refers to pictures you've shot with the iPhone, as opposed to pictures from your computer. Here again, you see the table of contents showing your iPhone shots.

The Camera Roll screen shows, at the bottom, how many pictures you've taken so far. To see one at full-screen size, tap it.

Once you've opened up a photo at full-screen size, a control bar appears briefly at the bottom of the screen. (If you don't see it, tap the screen again.)

The control bar includes the same icons described on page 95—🖼, ◀, ▶, and ➡—and one bonus icon: the Trash can (🗑). That's because, while you can't delete any of your *computer's* photos from the iPhone, you *can* delete pictures you've taken with the iPhone.

 Note For details on copying your iPhone photography back to your Mac or PC, see page 215.

6 | Getting Online

The iPhone's concept as an all-screen machine is a curse and a blessing. You may curse it when you're trying to type text, wishing you had real keys. But when you're online—oh, baby. That's when the Web comes to life, looming larger and clearer than on any other cellphone. That's when you see real email, full-blown YouTube videos, hyper-clear Google maps, and all kinds of Internet goodness, larger than life.

Well, at least larger than other cellphones.

Fortunately, you can use the Internet features of the iPhone as much as you want without worrying about price. Wi-Fi is free, and your AT&T plan includes unlimited use of the EDGE network.

A Tale of Two Networks

The iPhone is capable of getting online using either of two methods (which is one more than most phones):

- **Wi-Fi hot spots.** Wi-Fi, known to the geeks as 802.11 and to Apple fans as AirPort, means wireless networking. It's the same technology that lets laptops the world over get online at high speed in any Wi-Fi *hot spot*. Hot spots are everywhere these days: in homes, offices, coffee shops (notably Starbucks), hotels, airports, and thousands of other places.

 At *www.jiwire.com*, you can type an address or a city and find out exactly where to find the closest Wi-Fi hot spots. Or, quicker yet: Open Maps on your iPhone and type in, for example, *wifi austin* tx or *wifi 06902*. Pushpins on the map show you the closest Wi-Fi hot spots.

When you're in a Wi-Fi hot spot, your iPhone has a very fast connection to the Internet, as though it's connected to a cable modem or DSL.

Better yet, when you're online this way, you can make phone calls and surf the Internet simultaneously. And why not? Your iPhone has two independent antennas—one for Wi-Fi, and one for the cell network.

- **AT&T's cellular network.** Unfortunately, the whole world is not yet a Wi-Fi hot spot. Whenever you're outdoors, in a taxi, or otherwise in a non-Wi-Fied area, you have a Plan B to fall back on: AT&T's own cellular network. That is, your iPhone can connect to the data over the same airwaves that carry your voice.

The problem with the AT&T data network (called the EDGE network), of course, is that it's slow. Really slow—sometimes dial-up slow. And you can't be on a phone call while you're online using EDGE.

 AT&T also has a much faster data network—its so-called "3G" (third-generation) network. But it's available only in 160 U.S. cities so far, and the chips required to receive it draw an enormous amount of battery power. For those reasons, Apple designed the iPhone to use the older, slower network until the newer, faster one, and the chips necessary to receive it, improve.

Just how much faster is Wi-Fi than EDGE? Well, network speeds are measured in kilobits per second (which isn't the same as the more familiar kilo*bytes* per second; divide by 8 to get those).

AT&T's EDGE network is supposed to deliver anywhere from 70 to 200 kbps; a Wi-Fi hot spot is capable of delivering 6,500 to 2,100 kbps. You'll never get speeds near the high ends of those ranges—but even so, you can see that there's quite a difference.

The bottom line: getting online via Wi-Fi is *awesome*, and getting online via EDGE is…well, not so much. That's why the iPhone always prefers, and hops onto, a Wi-Fi connection when it's available.

Sequence of Connections

The iPhone isn't online all the time. To save battery power, it actually opens the connection only on demand: when you check email, request a Web page, open the YouTube program, and so on. At that point, the iPhone tries to get online following this sequence:

- First, it sniffs around for a Wi-Fi network that you've used before. If it finds one, it connects quietly and automatically. You're not asked for permission, a password, or anything else.

- If the iPhone can't find a previous hot spot, but it detects a *new* hot spot, a message appears on the screen. It displays the new hot spot's name; tap it to connect. (If you see a 🔒 icon next to the hot spot's name, then it's been protected by a password, which you'll have to enter.)

- If the iPhone can't find any Wi-Fi hot spots to join, or if you don't join any, it reluctantly connects to the cellular EDGE network. You won't win any speed competitions, but at least you'll be able to get online.

 Note Well, *usually* you'll get online. The EDGE network is available almost anywhere you can make a voice call. You'll know when you're connected to EDGE because a ᴇ icon appears on the phone's status bar. (When you're on via Wi-Fi, by contrast, you see 🛜 there instead.)

Silencing the "Want to Join?" Messages

Every now and then, you might be bombarded by those "Do you want to join?" messages, at a time when you have no need to be online. You might want the iPhone to stop bugging you—to *stop* offering Wi-Fi hot spots.

In that situation, from the Home screen, tap Settings→Wi-Fi and turn off Ask to Join Networks. When this option is off, then the iPhone never interrupts

your work by bounding in, wagging, and dropping the name of a new network at your feet. You always have to visit this Settings screen and select a network each time you want to go online, as described next.

The List of Hot Spots

At some street corners in big cities, Wi-Fi signals bleeding out of apartment buildings sometimes give you a choice of 20 or 30 hot spots to join. But whenever the iPhone invites you to join a hot spot, it suggests only one: the one with the strongest signal and, if possible, no password requirement.

But you might sometimes want to see the complete list of available hot spots—maybe because the iPhone-suggested hot spot is flaky. To see the full list, from the Home screen, tap Settings→Wi-Fi. Tap the one you want to join, as shown on the facing page.

Commercial Hot Spots

Tapping the name of the hot spot you want to join is generally all you have to do—if it's a home Wi-Fi network. Unfortunately, joining a *commercial* Wi-Fi hot spot—one that requires a credit-card number (in a hotel room or airport,

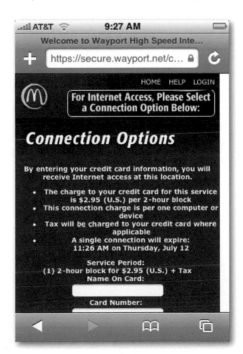

for example)—requires more than just connecting to it. You also have to *sign into* it, exactly as you'd do if you were using a laptop.

To do that, return to the Home screen and open Safari. You'll see the "Enter your payment information" screen either immediately, or as soon as you try to open a Web page of your choice.

Supply your credit-card information or (if you have a membership to this Wi-Fi chain, like Boingo or T-Mobile) your name and password. Click Submit or Proceed, try *not* to contemplate how this $8 per hour is pure profit for somebody, and enjoy your surfing.

Turning Off the Antennas—and Airplane Mode

To save battery power, and (on a plane) to comply with flight regulations, you can turn off one or both of the iPhone's antennas: Wi-Fi and cellular.

- **To turn Wi-Fi on or off.**
  From the Home screen, tap Settings→Wi-Fi. Tap the On/Off switch to shut this radio down (or turn it back on).

- **To turn both antennas off.**
  When you turn on Airplane mode (tap Settings, then turn on Airplane Mode), you turn off *both* the Wi-Fi *and* the cellular antennas. Now you can't make calls or get onto the Internet at all. You're saving battery power, however, and also complying with flight regulations that ban cellphones and other transmitters.

Once you're in Airplane mode, anything you do that requires voice or Internet access—text messages, Web, email, Weather, Stocks, Google Maps, and so on—triggers a message. "You must disable Airplane mode to access data." Tap either Cancel (to back out of your decision) or Disable (to turn off Airplane mode, turn on the antennas, and get online).

Note In the Safari Web browser, the message says, "Safari can't open the page because it can't find the server," but it's saying the same thing: No Can Connect to Internet Now, Boss.

You can, however, enjoy all the other iPhone features: use its iPod features, work with the camera and photos, or use any of the mini-programs like Clock, Calculator, and Notes. You can also work with stuff you've *already* downloaded to the phone, like email and voicemail messages.

7 The Web

T he Web on the iPhone looks like the Web on your computer, and that's one of Apple's greatest accomplishments. You see the real deal—the actual fonts, graphics, and layouts—not the stripped-down, bare-bones mini-Web you usually get on cellphone screens.

Treo

iPhone

The iPhone's Web browser is Safari, a lite version of the same one that comes with every Macintosh and is now available for Windows. It's fast (at least in a Wi-Fi hot spot), simple to use, and very pretty indeed.

Safari Tour

You get onto the Web by tapping the Safari icon on the Home screen (below, left); the very first time you do this, a blank browser window appears (below, right). As noted in the last chapter, the Web on the iPhone can be either speedy and satisfying (when you're in a Wi-Fi hot spot) or slow and excruciating (when you're on AT&T's cellular network). Even so, some Web is usually better than no Web at all.

> **Tip** You don't have to wait for a Web page to load entirely. You can zoom in, scroll, and begin reading the text even when only part of the page has appeared.

Safari has most of the features of a desktop Web browser: bookmarks, auto-complete (for Web addresses), bookmarks, cookies, a pop-up ad blocker, and so on. (It's missing niceties like password memorization and streaming music.)

Here's a quick tour of the main screen elements, starting from the upper left:

+ (Add Bookmark). When you're on a page that you might want to visit again later, bookmark it by tapping this button. Details on page 121.

- **Address bar.** This empty white box is where you enter the *URL* (Web address) for a page you want to visit. (URL is short for the even less self-explanatory Uniform Resource Locator.) See page 118.

✕, ↻ (Stop, Reload). Click the ✕ button to interrupt the download-ing of a Web page you've just requested (if you've made a mistake, for instance, or if it's taking too long).

Once a page has finished loading, the ✕ button turns into a ↻ button. Click this circular arrow if a page doesn't look or work quite right, or if you want to see the updated version of a Web page (such as a breaking-news site) that changes constantly. Safari re-downloads the Web page and reinterprets its text and graphics.

◄, ► (Back, Forward). Tap the ◄ button to revisit the page you were just on.

Once you've tapped ◄, you can then tap the ► button to return to the page you were on *before* you tapped the ◄ button.

⌘ (Bookmarks). This button brings up your list of saved bookmarks (page 121).

⎙, ⎙ (Page Juggler). Safari can keep multiple Web pages open, just like any other browser. Page 129 has the details.

> **Tip** When you're holding the iPhone the wide way (landscape orientation), you may have trouble tapping the buttons at the bottom of the screen (◄ ► ⌘ ⎙). That's because the chrome metal bezel supporting the screen makes the glass less tap-sensitive. Aim your taps slightly higher, away from the chrome, for better results.

Zooming and Scrolling

These two gestures—zooming in on Web pages and then scrolling around them—have probably sold more people on the iPhone than any other dem-onstration. It all happens with a fluid animation, and a responsiveness to your finger taps, that's positively addicting. Some people spend all day just zoom-ing in and out of Web pages on the iPhone, simply because they can.

When you first open a Web page, you get to see the *entire thing*. Unlike most cellphones, the iPhone crams the entire Web site onto its 3.5-inch screen, so you can get the lay of the land.

At this point, of course, you're looking at .004-point type, which is too small to read unless you're a microbe. So the next step is to magnify the *part* of the page you want to read.

The iPhone offers three ways to do that:

- **Rotate the iPhone.** Turn the device 90 degrees in either direction. The iPhone rotates and magnifies the image to fill the wider view.

- **Do the two-finger spread.** Put two fingers on the glass and drag them apart. The Web page stretches before your very eyes, growing larger. Then you can pinch to shrink the page back down again. (Most people do several spreads or several pinches in a row to achieve the degree of zoom they want.)

- **Double-tap.** Safari is intelligent enough to recognize different *chunks* of a Web page. One article might represent a chunk. A photograph might qualify as a chunk. When you double-tap a chunk, Safari magnifies *just that chunk* to fill the whole screen. It's smart and useful.

  Double-tap again to zoom back out.

Double-tap

Once you've zoomed out to the proper degree, you can then scroll around the page by dragging or flicking with a finger. You don't have to worry about "clicking a link" by accident; if your finger's in motion, Safari ignores the tapping action, even if you happen to land on a link.

It's awesome.

Tip Every now and then, you'll find, on a certain Web page, a *frame* (a column of text) with its own scroll bar—an area that scrolls independently of the main page. (If you have an Apple .mac account, for example, the Messages list is such a frame.)

The iPhone has a secret, undocumented method for scrolling one of these frames without scrolling the whole page: the *two-finger drag.* Check it out.

The Address Bar

As on a computer, this Web browser offers four ways to navigate the Web:

- Type an address into the Address bar.

- Choose a bookmark.

- Return to a site you've visited recently, using the History list.

- Tap a link.

These pages cover each of these methods in turn.

Tap anywhere on this strip...   *...to jump back to the top.*

 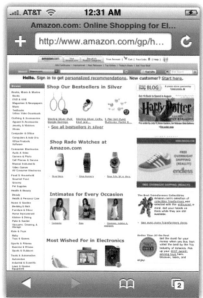

The Address bar is the strip at the top of the screen where you type in a Web page's address. And it so happens that *three* of the iPhone's greatest tips and shortcuts all have to do with this important navigational tool:

- **Insta-scroll to the top.** You can jump directly to the Address bar, no matter how far down a page you've scrolled, just by tapping the very top edge of the screen (on the status bar). That "tap the top" trick is timely, too, when a Web site *hides* the Address bar.

- **Don't delete.** There *is* a ⊗ button at the right end of the Address bar, whose purpose is to erase the entire current address so you can type another one. (Tap inside the Address bar to make it, and the keyboard, appear.) But the ⊗ button is for suckers.

  Instead, whenever the Address is open for typing, *just type*. Forget that there's already a URL there—just start typing. The iPhone is smart enough to figure out that you want to *replace* that Web address with a new one.

- **Don't type** *http://www or .com.* Safari is smart enough to know that most Web addresses use that format—so you can leave all that stuff out, and it will supply them automatically. Instead of *http://www.cnn.com*, for example, you can just type *cnn* and hit Go. (If it's .net, .org, or any other suffix, you have to type it.)

Otherwise, this Address bar works just like the one in any other Web browser. Tap inside it to make the keyboard appear. (If the Address bar is hidden, tap the top edge of the iPhone screen.)

The Safari Keyboard

In Safari, the keyboard works just as described on page 20, with three exceptions.

First, Safari is the only spot on the iPhone where you can *rotate* the keyboard into landscape orientation, as shown on the next page. This is a big deal; when it's stretched out the wide way, you get much bigger, broader keys, and typing is much easier and faster. Just remember to rotate the iPhone *before* you tap into the Address bar or text box; once the keyboard is on the screen, you can't rotate the image.

Second, there are no spaces allowed in Internet addresses; therefore, in the spot usually reserved for the Space bar, this keyboard has three keys for things that *do* appear often in Web addresses: period, /, and ".com."These nifty special keys make typing Web addresses a lot faster (below, left).

Third, tap the blue Go key when you're finished typing the address. That's your Enter key. (Or tap Done to hide the keyboard *without* "pressing Enter.")

As you type, a handy list of suggestions appears beneath the Address bar (below, right). These are all Web addresses that Safari already knows about, either because they're in your Bookmarks list or in your History list (meaning

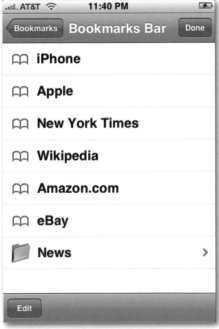

you've visited them recently). If you recognize the address you're trying to type, by all means tap it instead of typing out the rest of the URL. The time you save could be your own.

 Tip There's no Copy and Paste on the iPhone, but you *can* send the URL of an open Web page to a friend by email. When the Address bar is open for editing, a Share button appears above and to the left of it. Tap Share to switch into the iPhone's Mail program, where a new, outgoing message appears. The Subject line and body are already filled in (with the Web page's title and URL). All you have to do is address the message and send it. (Return to Safari by pressing Home→Safari.)

Bookmarks

Amazingly enough, Safari comes prestocked with bookmarks (Favorites)—that is, tags that identify Web sites you might want to visit again without having to remember and type their URLs. Even more amazingly, all of these canned bookmarks are interesting and useful to *you* in particular! How did it know?

Easy—it copied your existing desktop computer's browser bookmarks from Internet Explorer (Windows) or Safari (Macintosh) when you synced the iPhone (Chapter 11). Sneaky, eh?

Anyway, to see them, tap the 🕮 button at the bottom of the screen. You see

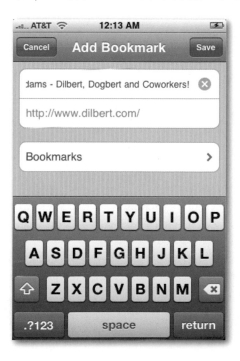

the master list of bookmarks. Some may be "loose," and many more are probably organized into folders, or even folders *within* folders. Tapping a folder shows you what's inside, and tapping a bookmark immediately begins opening the corresponding Web site.

Creating New Bookmarks

You can add new bookmarks right on the phone. Any work you do here is copied *back* to your computer the next time you sync the two machines.

When you find a Web page you might like to visit again, tap the **+** button (upper-left of the screen). The Add Bookmark screen appears. You have two tasks here:

- **Type a better name.** In the top box, you can type a shorter or clearer name for the page than the one it comes with. Instead of "Bass, Trout, & Tackle—the Web's Premiere Resource for the Avid Outdoorsman," you can just call it "Fish site."

  The box below this one identifies the underlying URL, which is totally independent from what you've *called* your bookmark. You can't edit this one.

- **Specify where to file this bookmark.** If you tap the button that says Bookmarks >, you open Safari's hierarchical list of bookmark folders, which organize your bookmarked sites. Tap the folder where you want to file the new bookmark, so you'll know where to find it later.

 Here's a site worth bookmarking: *http://google.com/gwt/n*. It gives you a bare-bones, superfast version of the Web, provided by Google for the benefit of people on slow connections (like EDGE). You can even opt to hide graphics for even more speed. Yeah, the iPhone's browser is glorious and all—but sometimes you'd rather have fast than pretty.

Editing Bookmarks and Folders

It's easy enough to massage your Bookmarks list—to delete favorites that aren't so favorite any more, make new folders, rearrange the list, rename a folder or a bookmark, and so on.

The techniques are the same for editing bookmark *folders* and editing the bookmarks themselves—after the first step. To edit the folder list, start by opening the Bookmarks list (tap the Ⱉ button), and then tap Edit.

To edit the bookmarks themselves, tap the Ⱉ button, tap a folder, and *then* tap Edit.

Now you can:

- **Delete something.** Tap the ⊖ button next to a folder or bookmark, and then tap Delete to confirm.

- **Rearrange the list.** Drag the grip strip (≡) up or down in the list to move the folders or bookmarks up or down. (You can't move or delete the top three folders—History, Bookmarks Bar, and Bookmarks Menu.)

- **Edit a name and location.** Tap a folder or bookmark name. If you tapped a folder, you arrive at the Edit Folder screen, which lets you edit the folder's name and which folder it's *inside* of. If you tapped a bookmark, you see the Edit Bookmark screen, where you can edit the name

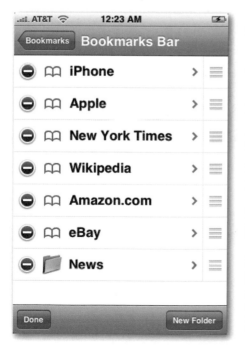
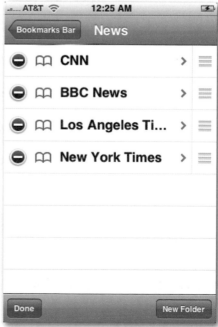

and the URL it points to. (It looks just like the Add Bookmark screen shown on page 121.)

Tap the Back button (upper-left corner) when you're finished.

- **Create a folder.** Tap the New Folder button in the lower-right corner of the Edit Folders screen. You're offered the chance to type a name for it and to specify where you want to file it (that is, in which *other* folder).

Tap Done when you're finished.

History List

Behind the scenes, Safari keeps track of the Web sites you've visited in the last week or so, neatly organized into subfolders like Earlier Today and Yesterday. It's a great feature when you can't recall the URL for a Web site that you visited recently—or when you remember that it had a long, complicated address and you get the psychiatric condition known as iPhone Keyboard Dread.

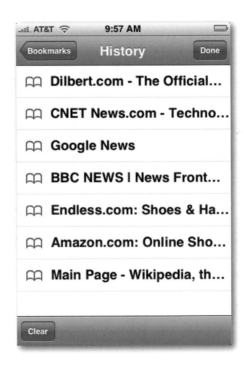

To see the list of recent sites, tap the 🕮 button, and then tap the History folder, whose icon bears a little clock to make sure you know that it's special.

Once the History list appears, just tap a bookmark (or a folder name and *then* a bookmark) to revisit that Web page.

Erasing the History List

Some people find it creepy that Safari maintains a complete list of every Web site they've seen recently, right there in plain view of any family member or coworker who wanders by. They'd just as soon their wife/husband/boss/parent/kid not know what Web sites they've been visiting.

You can't delete just one particularly incriminating History listing. You can, however, delete the *entire* History menu, thus erasing all of your tracks. To do that, tap Clear; confirm by tapping Clear History.

You've just rewritten History.

Tapping Links

You'd be surprised at the number of iPhone newbies who stare dumbly at the screen, awestruck at the beauty of full-blown Web pages—but utterly baffled as to how to click links.

The answer: Tap with your finger.

Here's the fourth and final method of navigating the Web: tapping links on the screen, much the way you'd click them if you had a mouse. As you know from desktop-computer browsing, not all links are blue and underlined. Sometimes, in fact, they're graphics.

The only difference is that on the iPhone, not all links take you to other Web pages. If you tap an email address, it opens up the iPhone's Mail program (Chapter 8) and creates a pre-addressed outgoing message. If you tap a phone number you find online, the iPhone calls it for you. There's even such a thing as a *map* link, which opens up the Google Maps program (page 175).

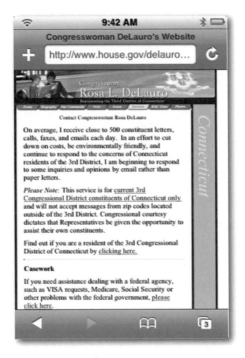

Each of these links, in other words, takes you out of Safari. If you want to return to your Web browsing, you have to tap Home→Safari. The page you had open is still there, waiting.

 Tip If you hold your finger on a link for a moment—touching rather than tapping—a handy bubble sprouts from it, identifying the full Web address that will open. For example, the link might *say,* "For a good time, click here," but it might actually take you to a Web site like *www.missingmanuals.com*.

Searching the Web

You might have noticed that whenever the Address bar appears, so does a Search bar just beneath it. (It's marked by a magnifying-glass icon that looks like ⚲ that.)

That's an awfully handy shortcut. It means that you can perform a Google search without having to go to Google.com first. Just tap into that box, type your search phrase, and then tap the big blue Google box in the corner.

Actually, you can tell the iPhone to use Yahoo's search feature instead of Google, if you like. From the Home screen, tap Settings→Safari→Search Engine.

Audio and Video on the Web

In general, streaming audio and video on the iPhone is a bust. The iPhone doesn't recognize the Real or Windows Media file formats, and the initial version doesn't understand Flash. All of this means that the iPhone can't play the huge majority of online video and audio recordings. That's a crushing disappointment to news and sports junkies.

But the iPhone isn't **utterly** clueless about streaming online goodies. It can play some QuickTime movies, like movie trailers, as long as they've been encoded (prepared) in certain formats (like H.264).

It can also play MP3 audio files right off the Web. That can be extremely handy for people who like to know what's going on in the world, because many European news agencies offer streaming MP3 versions of their news broadcasts. Here are a few worth bookmarking:

- **BBC News.** You can find five-minute news bulletins here. *www.bbc.co.uk/worldservice/programmes/newssummary.shtml*

- **Deutsche Welle.** English-language news, sports, arts, and talk from Germany. *www.dw-world.de/dw/0,2142,4703,00.html*

- **Radio France.** English-language broadcasts from France. *www.rfi.fr/langues/statiques/rfi_anglais.asp*

- **Voice of America.** The official external radio broadcast of the U.S. government. *www.voanews.com/english/*

Actually, any old MP3 files play fine right in Safari. If you've already played through your four or eight gigabytes of music from your computer, you can always do a Web search for *free mp3 music*.

Manipulating Multiple Pages

Like any self-respecting browser, Safari can keep multiple pages open at once, making it easy for you to switch between them. You can think of it as a miniature version of tabbed browsing, a feature of browsers like Safari Senior,

Firefox, and the latest Internet Explorer, which keeps a bunch of Web pages open simultaneously—in a single, neat window.

The beauty of this arrangement is that you can start reading one Web page while the others load into their own tabs in the background.

On the iPhone, it works like this:

- **To open a new window,** tap the ⬚ button in the lower-right. The Web page shrinks into a mini version. Tap New Page to open a new, untitled Web-browser tab; now you can enter an address, use a bookmark, or whatever.

 Note Sometimes, Safari sprouts a new window *automatically* when you click a link. That's because the link you tapped is programmed to open a new window. To return to the original window, read on.

- **To switch back to the first window,** tap ⬚ again. Now there are two dots (• •) beneath the miniature page, indicating that *two* windows are open. (The boldest, whitest dot indicates where you are in the horizontal row of windows.) Bring the first window's miniature onto the screen by flicking horizontally with your finger. Tap it to open it full-screen.

You can open a third window, and a fourth, and so on, and jump between them, using these two techniques. The icon sprouts a number to let you know how many windows are open; for example, it might say .

- **To close a window,** tap . Flick over to the miniature window you want to close, and then tap the button at its top-left corner.

 Note You can't close the very last window. Safari requires at least one window to be open.

Pop-up Blocker

The world's smarmiest advertisers have begun inundating us with pop-up and pop-under ads—nasty little windows that appear in front of the browser window, or, worse, behind it, waiting to jump out the moment you close your window. They're often deceptive, masquerading as error messages or dialog boxes, and they'll do absolutely anything to get you to click inside them.

Fortunately for you, Safari comes set to block those pop-ups so you don't see them. It's a war out there—but at least you now have some ammunition.

The thing is, though, pop-ups are sometimes legitimate (and not ads)—notices of new banking features, seating charts on ticket-sales sites, warnings that the instructions for using a site have changed, and so on. Safari can't tell these from ads—and it stifles them too. So if a site you trust says "Please turn off pop-up blockers and reload this page," you know you're probably missing out on a *useful* pop-up message.

In those situations, you can turn off the pop-up blocker. From the Home screen, tap Settings→Safari. Where it says "Block Pop-ups," tap the On/Off switch.

Cookies, Cache, and Other Security Options

Cookies are something like Web page preference files. Certain Web sites—particularly commercial ones like Amazon.com—deposit them on your hard drive like little bookmarks, so they'll remember you the next time you visit. Ever notice how Amazon.com greets you "Welcome, Chris" (or whatever your name is)? It's reading its own cookie, left behind on your hard drive (or in this case, on your iPhone).

Most cookies are perfectly innocuous—and, in fact, are extremely helpful, because they help Web sites remember your tastes. Cookies also spare you the effort of having to type in your name, address, and so on, every time you visit these Web sites.

But fear is widespread, and the media fans the flames with tales of sinister cookies that track your movement on the Web. If you're worried about invasions of privacy, Safari is ready to protect you.

To check all this out, from the Home screen, tap Settings→Safari. The options here are like a paranoia gauge. If you click Never, you create an acrylic shield around your iPhone. No cookies can come in, and no cookie information can go out. You'll probably find the Web a very inconvenient place; you'll have to re-enter your information upon every visit, and some Web sites may not work properly at all. The Always option means, "oh, what the heck—just gimme all of them."

A good compromise is From Visited, which accepts cookies from sites you *want* to visit, but blocks cookies deposited on your hard drive by sites you're not actually visiting—cookies an especially evil banner ad gives you, for example.

This screen also offers a Clear Cookies button (deletes all the cookies you've accumulated so far), as well as Clear History (page 125) and Clear Cache.

The *cache* is a little patch of the iPhone's storage area where bits and pieces of Web pages you visit—graphics, for example—are retained. The idea is that the next time you visit the same page, the iPhone won't have to download those bits again. It's already got them on board, so the page appears much faster.

If you worry that your cache eats up space, poses a security risk, or is confusing some page (and preventing the most recent version of the page from appearing), tap this button to erase it and start over.

RSS: The Missing Manual

In the beginning, the Internet was an informational Garden of Eden. There were no banner ads, pop-ups, flashy animations, or spam messages. Back then, people thought the Internet was the greatest idea ever.

Those days, alas, are long gone. Web browsing now entails a constant battle against intrusive advertising and annoying animations. And with the proliferation of Web sites of every kind—from news sites to personal weblogs (*blogs*)—just reading your favorite sites can become a full-time job.

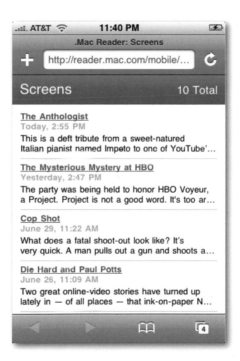

Enter RSS, a technology that lets you subscribe to *feeds*—summary blurbs provided by thousands of sources around the world, from Reuters to Apple to your nerdy next-door neighbor. The result: You spare yourself the tediousness of checking for updates manually, plus you get to read short summaries of new articles without ads and blinking animations. And if you want to read a full article, you just tap its headline.

 Note RSS either stands for Rich Site Summary or Really Simple Syndication. Each abbreviation explains one aspect of RSS—either its summarizing talent or its simplicity.

Safari, as it turns out, doubles as a handy RSS reader. Whenever you tap an "RSS Feed" link on a Web page, or whenever you type the address of an RSS feed into the Address bar (it often begins with *feed://*), Safari automatically displays a handy table-of-contents view that lists all of the news blurbs on that page.

Scan through the summaries—and when you see an article that looks intriguing, tap its headline. You go to the full-blown Web page to read the full-blown article.

 Tip It's worth bookmarking your favorite RSS feeds. One great one for tech fans is *feed://www.digg.com/rss/index.xml*, a constantly updated list of the coolest and most interesting tech and pop-culture stories of the day. Most news publications offer news feeds, too. (Your humble author's own daily *New York Times* blog has a feed that's *http://pogue.blogs.nytimes.com/?feed=rss2*.)

8 Email

You ain't never seen email on a phone like this. It offers full formatting, fonts, graphics, choice of type size; file attachments like Word, Excel, PDF, and photos; compatibility with Yahoo Mail, Gmail, AOL Mail, .Mac mail, and just about any standard email account. Dude, if you want a more satisfying portable email machine than this one, buy a laptop.

Setting Up Your Account

If you play your cards right, you won't *have* to set up your email account on the phone. The first time you set up the iPhone to sync with your computer (Chapter 11), you're offered the chance to *sync* your Mac's or PC's mail with the phone. That doesn't mean it copies actual messages—only the email settings, so the iPhone is ready to start downloading mail.

You're offered this option if your Mac's mail program is Mail or Microsoft Entourage, or if your PC's mail program is Outlook or Outlook Express.

But what if you don't use one of those email programs? No sweat. You can also plug the necessary settings right into the iPhone.

Free Email Accounts

If you have a free (or paid) email account from Google, AOL, Yahoo, or .Mac, setup on the iPhone is easy.

From the Home screen, tap Settings→Mail→Add Account. Tap the colorful logo that corresponds to the kind of account you have (Google, Yahoo, or whatever).

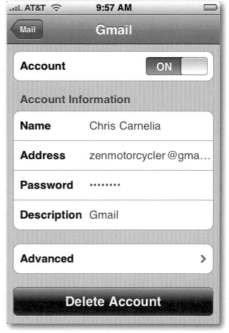

Now you land on the account-information screen. Tap into each of the four blanks and, when the keyboard appears, type your name, email address, account password, and a description (that one's optional). Tap Save.

Your email account is ready to go!

 Tip If you don't have one of these free accounts, they're worth having, if only as a backup to your regular account. They can help with spam filtering, too, since the iPhone doesn't offer any; see page 154. To sign up, go to Google.com, Yahoo.com, AOL.com, or Mac.com.

POP3, IMAP, and Exchange Accounts

Those freebie, Web-based accounts are super-easy to set up. But they're not the whole ball of wax. Millions of people have one of these more commercial, corporate email accounts, perhaps supplied by their employers or Internet providers:

- **POP accounts** are extremely common on the Internet. (It stands for Post Office Protocol, but this won't be on the test.)

   A POP server transfers your incoming mail to your computer (or iPhone) before you read it, which works fine as long as you're using only that machine to access your email.

- **IMAP accounts** (Internet Message Access Protocol) are newer and have more features than POP servers, but aren't as common. IMAP servers keep all of your mail online, rather than making you store it on your computer; as a result, you can access the same mail regardless of the computer (or phone) you use. IMAP servers remember which messages you've read and sent, too. (Those free Yahoo email accounts are IMAP accounts, and so are Apple's .Mac accounts.)

   One downside to this approach, of course, is that you can't delete your email—or read it for the first time—unless you're online, because all of your mail is on an Internet server. Another disadvantage is that if you don't conscientiously manually delete mail after you've read it, your online mailbox eventually overflows. Sooner or later, the system starts bouncing new messages back to their senders, annoying your friends.

Tip You can ask the iPhone to copy your IMAP messages onto the phone itself, so you can work on your email even when you're not online. From the Home screen, tap Settings→Mail→your IMAP account name→Advanced→Drafts Mailbox. Under On My Phone, tap Drafts. Go back one screen and repeat with the Sent Mailbox and Deleted Mailbox items.

- **Exchange servers** are central email hubs that are popular in corporations and some schools. Most of the time, employees tap into these servers using a Windows email program like Outlook. Corporate tech types like Exchange servers because they're easy to set up and maintain, and because they offer many of the same features as IMAP servers.

The iPhone can communicate with all three kinds of accounts, with varying degrees of completeness.

If you haven't opted to have your account-setup information transferred automatically to the iPhone from your Mac or PC (page 224), then you can set it up manually on the phone.

From the Home screen, tap Settings→Mail→Add Account. Tap Other, and then tap the tab representing the kind of account you're setting up: POP, IMAP, or Exchange.

These account types require more setting up than the free Web accounts. Now you'll have to enter such juicy details as the Host Name for Incoming and Outgoing Mail servers. (There's even more geeky goodness on the Advanced screen: SSL, Authentication, IMAP Path Prefix, and so on.)

If you don't know this stuff offhand, you'll have to ask your Internet provider, corporate tech-support person, or next-door teenager to help you. Especially in the first version, the iPhone's mail-setup process can involve quite a bit of time and troubleshooting.

 The iPhone can't check corporate Exchange mail *unless* the system administrator can be persuaded to turn on the server's IMAP feature. That's probably going to be a hard sell at most security-conscious corporations.

There is hope, however. Visto (visto.com) plans to unveil a software package by the end of 2007 that, once installed by the system administrator, will allow the iPhone to connect to Exchange mail servers without sacrificing security. Start buttering up your company's geeks now.

When you're finished, tap Save.

The "Two-Mailbox Problem"

It's awesome that the iPhone can check the mail from a POP mail account, which is the sort provided by most Internet providers. This means, however, that now you've got *two* machines checking the same account—your main computer and your iPhone.

Now you've got the "two-mailbox problem." What if your computer downloads some of the mail, and your iPhone downloads the rest? Will your mail stash be awkwardly split between two machines? How will you remember where to find a particular message?

Fortunately, the problem is halfway solved by a factory setting deep within the iPhone that says, in effect: "The iPhone may download mail, but will leave a copy behind for your desktop computer to download later."

 If you must know, this setting is at Settings→Mail→account name→Advanced→ "Delete from server"→Never.

Unfortunately, that doesn't stop the opposite problem. It doesn't prevent the *computer* from downloading messages before your *iPhone* can get to them. When you're out and about, therefore, you may miss important messages.

Most people would rather not turn off the computer every time they leave the desk. Fortunately, there's a more automatic solution: turn on the "Leave messages on server" option in your Mac or PC email program. Its location depends on which email program you use. For example:

- **Entourage.** Choose Tools→Accounts. Double-click the account name; click Options. Turn on "Leave a copy of each message on the server."

> **Tip** Also turn on "Delete messages from the server after they are deleted from this computer," so that your iPhone won't wind up re-downloading messages you've already disposed of on your computer.

- **Mail.** Choose Mail→Preferencesl→Accountsl→account namel→ Advanced. Turn off "Remove copy from server after retrieving a message."

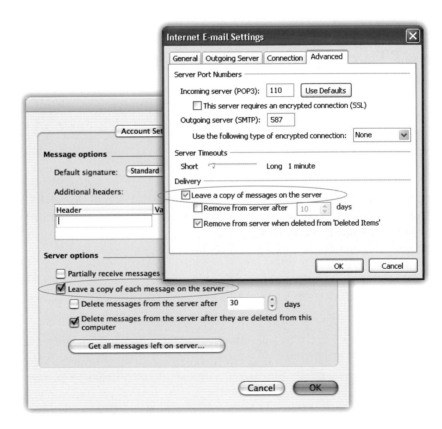

- **Outlook.** Choose Tools→E-mail Accounts→E-mail. Click "View or Change E-Mail Accounts"→Next→your account name→Change→More Settings→Advanced. Turn off "Leave a copy of messages on the server."

- **Outlook Express.** Choose Tools→Accounts→your account name→Properties→Advanced. Turn off "Leave a copy of messages on the server."

With this arrangement, both machines download the same mail; messages aren't deleted until you delete them from the bigger computer.

 Tip Here's another tip that may help : Turn on "Always Cc Myself" (in Settings→Mail). It ensures that when you send a message from your iPhone, it fires off a copy to your own email address—so that when you return to your desk, you'll have copies of all the messages you wrote from the road. (Yeah, they'll be in your Inbox and not your Sent Mail, but at least it's something.)

And explore the possibility of getting (or forwarding your mail to) an IMAP account like Yahoo Mail, which avoids this whole mess. Then whatever changes you make on one machine are magically reflected on the other.

Reading Mail

In general, your iPhone checks for new messages automatically every 15, 30, or 60 minutes, depending on your preferences (page 253), as well as each time you open the Mail program.

There are two notable exceptions:

- **Manual checking.** You can turn off automatic checking altogether. If, in Settings→Mail→Auto-Check, you choose Manual, then your iPhone won't check for new messages except when you tap the Check button (↻) within the Mail program.

- **Real-time delivery.** If you have a free Yahoo Mail account, you get a delicious perk: *real-time* email delivery. That's also called "push" email, well known to BlackBerry addicts; it means that new messages show up on your iPhone *as they arrive*.

  There's nothing to turn on here, no options; if you have a Yahoo Mail account, your messages show up as they arrive, automatically. (Yahoo mail, as noted earlier, is also an IMAP account, meaning that when you send, file, or delete a message on your phone, you'll find those changes reflected at Yahoo.com.)

When new mail arrives, you'll know it by a glance at your Home screen, because the Mail icon sprouts a circled number that tells you how many new messages are waiting. You'll also hear the iPhone's little "You've got mail" sound, unless you've turned that off in Settings (page 254).

 Note If you have more than one email account, this number shows you the *total* number of new messages, from all accounts. The Accounts screen, shown below, shows the breakdown by account.

To read them, tap Mail. You return to whatever screen you had open the last time you were in Mail, which could be any of several things:

- **Accounts.** If you have more than one email account (corporate and personal, for example), they appear here in this master list. Tap one to drill down to the next screen, which is...

- **Mailboxes.** Here are the traditional mail folders: Inbox, Drafts (written but not sent), Sent, Trash, and any folders that you've created yourself (Family,

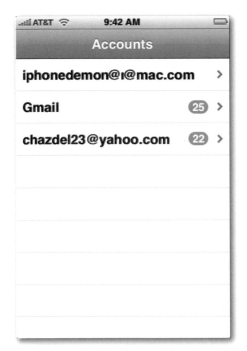
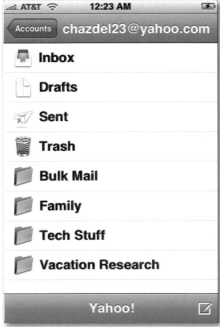

Little League, Old Stuff, whatever). If you have a Yahoo or IMAP account, these folders are automatically created on the iPhone to match what you've set up online.

 Note Not all kinds of email accounts permit the creation of your own filing folders, so you may not see anything but Inbox, Sent, and Trash.

Tap one of these folders to drill down into…

- **Mail list.** Here's where you see the subject lines of your messages. Each one reveals, in light gray type, the first few lines of its contents, so that you can scan through new messages and see if there's anything important. You can flick your finger to scroll this list, if it's long. Blue dots indicate messages you haven't yet opened.

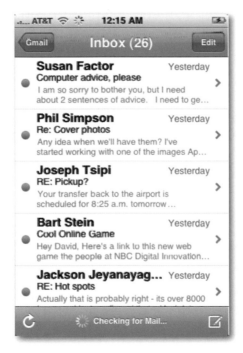

Finally, tap a message to open…

- **The message window.** Here, at last, is the actual, readable, scrollable message.

What to Do With a Message

Once you've viewed a message, you can respond to it, delete it, print it, file it, and so on. Here's the drill.

Read It

The type size in email messages can be pretty small. Fortunately, you have some great iPhoney enlargement tricks at your disposal. For example:

- **Spread two fingers** to enlarge the entire email message (page 18).

- **Double-tap a narrow block of text** to make it fill the screen, if it doesn't already.

Drag or flick your finger to scroll through or around the message.

> **Tip** You can also, of course, just ask the iPhone to use a larger type size. From the Home screen, tap Settings→Mail→Minimum Font Size. You can choose the minimum type size you want from these options: Small, Medium, Large, Extra Large, or Giant. (What, no Humongous?)

It's nice to note that links are "live" in email messages. Tap a phone number to call it; a Web address to open it; a YouTube link to watch it; an email address to write to it; and so on.

Reply to It

To answer a message, tap the Reply/Forward icon (◄) at the bottom of the screen. You're asked if you want to Reply or Forward; tap Reply. If the message was originally addressed to multiple recipients, you can send your reply to everyone simultaneously by clicking Reply All instead.

A new message window opens, already addressed. As a courtesy to your correspondent, Mail places the original message at the bottom of the window.

At this point, you can add or delete recipients, edit the Subject line or the original message, and so on.

Use the Return key to create blank lines in the original message. (Use the Loupe— page 23—to position the insertion point at the proper spot.)

Using this method, you can splice your own comments into the paragraphs of the original message, replying point by point. The brackets preceding each line of the original message help your correspondent keep straight what's yours and what's hers.

When you're finished, tap Send.

Forward It

Instead of replying to the person who sent you a message, you may sometimes want to pass the note on to a third person.

To do so, tap ← button at the bottom of the screen. This time, tap Forward.

 If there's a file attached to the inbound message, the iPhone says, "Include attachments from original message?" and offers Include/Don't Include buttons. Rather thoughtful, actually—the phone can pass on files that it can't even open.

A new message opens, looking a lot like the one that appears when you reply. You may wish to precede the original message with a comment of your own, along the lines of, "Frank: I thought you'd be interested in this joke about your mom."

Finally, address and send it as you would any outgoing piece of mail (page 150).

File It

As noted earlier, some mail accounts let you create filing folders to help manage your messages. Once you've opened a message that's worth keeping, you file it by tapping the ▣ button at the bottom of the screen. Up pops the list of your folders; tap the one you want.

Delete It

Sometimes it's junk mail. Sometimes you're just done with it. Either way, it's a snap to delete a message.

If the message is open on the screen before you, simply tap the ▥ button at the bottom of the screen. Frankly, it's worth deleting tons of messages just for the pleasure of watching the animation as they funnel down into that tiny icon, whose lid pops open and shut accordingly.

 Tip If that one-touch Delete method makes you a little nervous, you can ask the iPhone to display a confirmation box before trashing the message forever. See page 254.

You can also delete a message from the message *list*—the Inbox, for example. Just swipe your finger across the message listing, in either direction. (It doesn't have to be an especially broad swipe.) The red Delete button appears; tap it to confirm, or tap anywhere else if you change your mind.

There's a long way to delete messages from the list, too—tap Edit, tap ⊖, tap Delete, tap Done—but the finger-swipe method is *much* more fun.

 Note When you delete a message, it goes into the Deleted folder. In other words, it works like the Macintosh Trash or the Windows Recycle Bin. You have a safety net.

Email doesn't have to stay in the Deleted folder forever, however. You can ask the iPhone to empty that folder every day, week, or month. From the Home screen, tap Settings→Mail. Tap your account name, then Advanced→Remove. Now you can change the setting from "Never" to "After one day" (or week, or month).

Add the Sender to Contacts

If you get a message from someone new who's worth adding to your iPhone's Contacts address book, tap the blue, oval-shaded email address (where it says "From:"). You're offered two buttons: *Email* (meaning, "reply") and *Create New Contact*. Use that second button if you think you may one day want to write this person back.

Open an Attachment

The Mail program downloads and displays the icons for *any* kind of attachment—but it can *open* only Word, Excel, PDF, and graphics files. Just scroll to the bottom of the screen, tap the attachment's icon, and marvel as the document opens up, full-screen. You can zoom in and zoom out, flick, and scroll just as though it's a Web page or photo (page 91).

You just can't edit it.

When you're finished admiring the attachment, tap *Message* (top-left corner) to return to the original email message.

View the Details

When your computer's screen measures only 3.5 inches diagonally, there's not a lot of extra space. So Apple designed Mail to conceal the details that you might need only occasionally. They reappear, naturally enough, when you tap the blue word Details in the upper-right corner of a message.

Now you get to see a few more details about the message. For instance:

- **Who it's to.** Well, duh—it's to *you*, right?

  Yes, but it might have been sent to other people, too. When you open the Details, you see who else got this note—along with anyone who was CC'cd (sent a copy).

  Tip When you tap the person's name in the blue oval, you open the corresponding info card in Contacts. It contains one-touch buttons for calling someone back (tap the phone number) or sending a text message (tap Text Message)—which can be very handy if the email message you just received is urgent.

- **Mark as Unread.** In the Inbox, any message you haven't yet read is marked by a blue dot (●). Once you've opened the message, the blue dot goes away.

By tapping *Mark as Unread*, however, you make that blue dot **reappear**. It's a great way to flag a message for later, to call it to your own attention. The blue dot can mean not so much "unread" as "un-dealt with."

Tap *Hide* to collapse these details.

Move On

Once you've had a good look at a message and processed it to your satisfaction, you can move on to the next (or previous) message in the list by tapping the ▲ or ▼ button in the upper-right corner.

Or you can tap the Back button in the upper-left corner to return to the Inbox (or whatever mailbox you're in).

Writing Messages

To compose a new piece of outgoing mail, open the Mail program, and then tap the ☑ icon in the lower-right corner. A new, blank outgoing mail appears, and the iPhone keyboard pops up. Here's how you go about writing a message:

❶ **In the "To:" field, type the recipient's email address—or grab it from Contacts.** Often, you won't have to type much more than the first couple

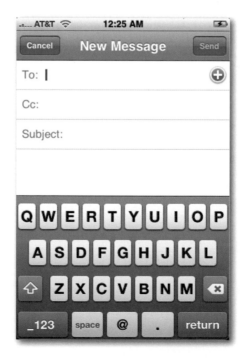

of letters of the name *or* email address. As you type, Mail automatically displays all the matching names and addresses, so that you can simply tap one instead of typing. (It thoughtfully derives these suggestions by analyzing both your Contacts *and* people you've recently exchanged email with.)

Alternatively, tap the ⊕ button to open your Contacts list. Tap the name of the person you want. (Note, though, that the Contacts list shows you *all* names, even those that don't have email addresses.)

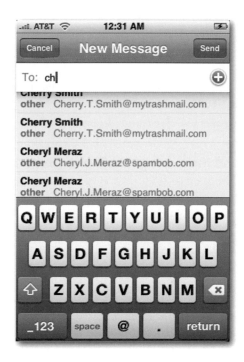

You can add as many addressees as you like; just repeat the addressing procedure over and over.

Tip There's no Group feature on the iPhone, which would let you send one message to a predefined set of friends. But at *http://groups.yahoo.com*, you can create free email groups. You can send a single email message to the group's address, and everyone in the group will get a copy. (You have to set up one of these groups in a Web browser—but lo and behold, your iPhone has one!)

---

❷ **To send a copy to other recipients, enter the address(es) in the "Cc:" field.** Cc stands for *carbon copy*. Getting an email message where your name is in the Cc line implies: "I sent you a copy because I thought you'd want to know about this correspondence, but I'm not expecting you to reply."

❸ **Type the topic of the message in the Subject field.** It's courteous to put some thought into the Subject line. (Use "Change in plans for next week," for instance, instead of "Yo.") And leaving it blank only annoys your recipient. On the other hand, don't put the *entire* message into the Subject line, either.

❹ **Type your message in the message box.** All the usual iPhone keyboard tricks apply (page 21).

 You can't attach anything to an outgoing message—at least not directly. You can email a photo from within the Photos program (page 97), though, and you can *forward* a file attached to an incoming piece of mail.

❺ **Tap Send (to send the message) or Cancel (to back out of it).** If you tap Cancel, the iPhone asks if you want to save the message. If you tap Save, the message lands in your Drafts folder. Tap the Back button (upper-left) a couple of times to see it.

Later, you can open the Drafts folder, tap the aborted message, finish it up and send it.

 If your iPhone refuses to send mail from your POP account, see page 274 for the geeky, but quick, solution.

The Fake Resend Command

The iPhone's Mail program doesn't have some of the features you may be used to—like a Resend command, which lets you open a message you've already sent so that you can send it again to somebody new.

But it *can* do a Resend—if you know the secret.

Open the Sent folder on your iPhone. Select the message you want to resend, tap the 🖻 icon, and tap the Drafts folder. You've just put the message back into the Drafts folder, where you can now open it, readdress it, and send!

Signatures

A *signature* is a bit of text that gets stamped at the bottom of your outgoing email messages. It can be your name, a postal address, or a pithy quote.

Unless you intervene, the iPhone stamps "Sent from my iPhone" at the bottom of every message. You may be just fine with that, or you may consider it the equivalent of gloating (or free advertising for Apple). In any case, you can change the signature if you want to.

From the Home screen, tap Settings→Mail→Signature. The Signature text window appears, complete with keyboard, so that you can compose the signature you want.

Surviving Email Overload

If you don't get much mail, you probably aren't lying awake at night, trying to think of ways to manage so much information overload on your tiny phone.

If you do get a lot of mail, here are some tips.

The Spam Problem

Mail is an awfully full-fledged email program for a *phone*. But compared with a desktop email program, it's really only half-fledged. You can't send file attachments, can't delete messages en masse, can't create mail rules, can't send a BCC (blind carbon copy) message—and can't screen out spam.

Spam, the junk mail that now makes up more than 80% of email, is a problem that's only getting worse. So how are you supposed to keep it off your iPhone?

The following solution will take 15 minutes to set up, but it will make you very happy in the long run.

Suppose your regular email address is *iphonecrazy@comcast.com*.

❶ **Sign up for a free Gmail account.** You do that at *www.gmail.com*.

The idea here is that you're going to have all your *iphonecrazy@comcast.com* messages sent on to this Gmail account, and you'll set up your iPhone to check the **Gmail** account instead of your regular account.

Why? Because Gmail has excellent spam filters. They'll clean up the mail mess before it reaches your iPhone.

Unfortunately, just **forwarding** your mail to the Google account won't do the trick. If you do that, then the return address on every message that reaches your iPhone will be *iphonecrazy@comcast.com*. When you tap Reply on the iPhone, your response won't be addressed to the original sender; it'll be addressed right back to you!

But the brainiacs at Google have anticipated this problem, too.

❷ **Sign in to Gmail. Click Settings→Accounts→"Add another email account," and fill in the email settings for your main address. Turn**

on "Leave a copy of retrieved message on the server." What you've just done is to tell Gmail to *fetch the mail* from your main address. The return addresses remain intact!

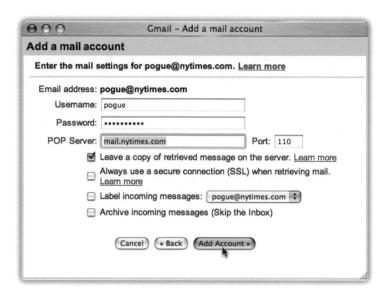

But it gets better. As you complete the setup process in Gmail, you'll see a message that says: "You can now retrieve mail from this account. Would you also like to be able to send mail as iphonecrazy@comcast.com?"

❸ **Click "Yes, I want to be able to send mail as [your real email address]."** In other words, your iPhone will not only *receive* spam-filtered mail from your main account—but when you reply, your main email address, not Gmail's, will be the return address!

Trying to figure all this out is like solving a Rubik's cube with your eyes closed. But here's the bottom line: although the iPhone is set up to check your *Gmail* account, Gmail is, at this point, only a spam-filtering go-between. All mail sent to your main address (*iphonecrazy@comcast.com*) will now come to your iPhone, and all responses from your iPhone will seem to have come from *iphonecrazy@comcast.com*.

And as an added, *added* bonus, you can now check your *iphonecrazy@ comcast.com* email from any computer that has a Web browser—at Gmail.com.

Next time, keep your email address out of spammers' hands in the first place. Use one address for the public areas of the Internet, like chat rooms, online shopping, Web site and software registration, and newsgroup posting. Spammers use automated software robots that scour these pages, recording email addresses they find. Create a separate email account for person-to-person email—and *never* post that address on a Web page.

Condensing the Message List

As you may have noticed, the messages in your In box are listed with the Subject line in bold type *and* a couple of lines, in light gray text, that preview the message itself.

You can control how many lines of the light gray preview text show up here. From the Home screen, tap Settings→Mail→Preview. Choosing *None* means you fit a lot more message titles on each screen without scrolling; choosing *5 lines* shows you a lot of each message, but means you'll have to do more scrolling.

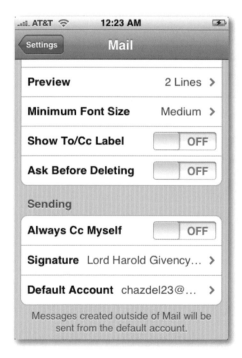
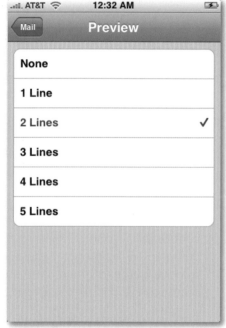

How Many Messages

On iPhone 1.0, there's no way to delete a bunch of messages at once. Yes, it's fun to delete messages with a horizontal finger swipe, but if you're used to a desktop email program, you may get stressed about having to do that one message at a time.

Instead, you may just want to get used to letting new messages push the old ones off the screen. In Settings→Mail→Show, you can specify how many messages you want to appear in the list before scrolling off the screen: 25, 50, 200, whatever.

It's only a false sense of being on top of things—you can always tap the "Load 25 More Messages" button to retrieve the next batch—but at least you'll never have a 2,000-message Inbox.

Spotting Worthwhile Messages

The iPhone can display a little **To** or **Cc** logo on each piece of mail in your Inbox. At a glance, it helps you identify which messages are actually intended for *you*. Messages without those logos are probably spam, newsletters, mailing lists, or other messages that weren't specifically addressed to you as a human being, and probably don't deserve your immediate attention.

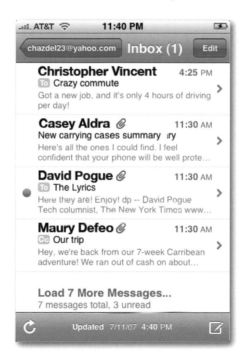

To turn on these little badges, visit Settings→Mail, and turn on "Show To/CC Label." There's virtually no downside to using this feature.

Managing Accounts

If you have more than one email account, you can turn them on and off at will. You might deactivate one for awhile because, for example, you don't plan to do much traveling for the next month.

You can also delete an account entirely.

All of this happens at Settings→Mail. When you see your list of accounts, tap the one you want. At the top of the screen, you'll see the On/Off switch, which you can use to make an account dormant. And at the bottom, you'll see the Delete Account button.

 Tip If you have several accounts, which one does the iPhone use when you send mail from within other programs—like when you email a photo from Photos or a link from Safari?

It uses the *default* account, of course. You determine which one is the default account in Settings→Mail (scroll to the very bottom).

Virtual Private Networking (VPN)

The typical corporate network is guarded by a team of steely-eyed administrators for whom Job Number One is preventing access by unauthorized visitors. They perform this job primarily with the aid of a super-secure firewall that seals off the company's network from the Internet.

So how can you tap into the network from the road? Only one solution is both secure and cheap: the *Virtual Private Network*, or VPN. Running a VPN lets you create a super-secure "tunnel" from your iPhone, across the Internet, and straight into your corporate network. All data passing through this tunnel is heavily encrypted. To the Internet eavesdropper, it looks like so much undecipherable gobbledygook.

VPN is, however, a corporate tool, run by corporate nerds. Your company's tech staff can tell you whether or not there's a VPN server set up for you to use.

If they do have one, then you'll need to know the type of server it is. The iPhone can connect to VPN servers that speak *PPTP* (Point to Point Tunneling Protocol) and *L2TP/IPsec* (Layer 2 Tunneling Protocol over the IP Security Protocol), both relatives of the PPP language spoken by modems. Most corporate VPN servers work with at least one of these protocols. (iPhone 1.0 can't connect to Cisco servers, although a software update may one day take care of that.)

To set up your VPN connection, visit Settings→General→Network→VPN. Tap the On/Off switch to make the VPN configuration screen pop up. Tap either L2TP or PPTP, depending on which kind of server your company uses. (Ask the network administrator.) The most critical bits of information to fill in are these:

- **Server.** The Internet address of your VPN server (for example, *vpn. ferrets-r-us.com*).

- **Account; Password.** Here's your user account name and password, as supplied by the IT guys.

 Note Some networks require that you type the currently displayed password on an **RSA SecurID card**, which your administrator will provide. This James Bondish, credit-card-like thing displays a password that changes every few seconds, making it rather difficult for hackers to learn "the" password.

- **Secret.** If your office offers L2TP connections, you'll need yet another password called a *Shared Secret* to ensure that the server you're connecting to is really the server that you intend to connect to.

Once you know everything's in place, the iPhone can connect to the corporate network and fetch your corporate mail. You don't have to do anything special on your end; everything works just as described in this chapter.

9

Maps and Apps

Your Home screen is loaded with goodies. Those 16 icons include major gateways to the Internet (Safari), critical communications tools (Phone, SMS, and Mail), visual records of your life (Photos, Camera), and a well-stocked entertainment center (iPod).

The other applications (apps) may not exactly be the legs that prop up the table of your life. But each one, in its way, will come in *extremely* handy at some point in your iPhone life.

This chunky chapter covers all of the smaller programs, from top to bottom of the Home screen: Calendar, YouTube, Stocks, Maps, Weather, Clock, Calculator, and Notes.

Calendar

What kind of digital companion would the iPhone be if it didn't have a calendar program? In fact, not only does it have a calendar—it even has one that syncs with your computer. If you maintain your life's schedule on a Mac (in iCal or Entourage) or a PC (in Outlook), then you've already got it on your iPhone. Make a change in one place, and it changes in the other.

See page 222 for details on setting up this two-way syncing.

But you can also use Calendar all by itself.

 Tip The Calendar icon on the Home screen shows what looks like one of those paper Page-a-Day calendar pads. But if you look closely, you'll see a sweet touch: It actually shows *today's* day and date!

Working with Views

By clicking one of the View buttons at the top of the screen, you can switch among these views:

- **List view** offers you a tidy chronological list of everything you've got going on, from today forward. Flick or drag your finger to scroll through it.

- **Day** shows the appointments for a single day in the main calendar area, broken down by time slot. Tap the ◀ and ▶ buttons to move backward or forward a day at a time.

> **Tip** *Hold down* one of the ◀ and ▶ buttons to zoom through the dates quickly. You can skip into a date next month in just a few seconds.

- **Month** shows the entire month. Little dots on the date squares show you when you're busy. Tap a date square to read, in the bottom part of the screen, what you've got going on that day. (You can flick or drag that list to scroll it.)

In all three views, you can tap the Today button (top left) to return to today's date.

Making an Appointment

The basic calendar is easy to figure out. After all, with the exception of one unfortunate Gregorian incident, we've been using calendars successfully for centuries.

Even so, recording an event on this calendar is quite a bit more flexible than entering one on, say, one of those "Hunks of the Midwest Police" paper calendars.

Start by tapping the ✚ button (top-right corner of the screen). The Add Event screen pops up, filled with tappable lines of information. Tap one (like Title/Location, Starts/Ends, or Repeat) to open a configuration screen for that element. For example:

- **Title/Location.** Name your appointment here. For example, you might type *Fly to Phoenix*.

  The second line, called *Location*, makes a lot of sense. If you think about it, almost everyone needs to record *where* a meeting is to take place. You might type a reminder for yourself like *My place*, a specific address like *212 East 23*, a contact phone number, or a flight number.

  Use the keyboard (page 20) as usual. When you're finished, tap Save.

- **Starts/Ends.** On this screen, tap *Starts*, and then indicate the starting time for this appointment, using the four spinning dials on the bottom half of the screen. The first sets the date; the second, the hour; the third, the minutes; the fourth, AM or PM. If only real alarm clocks were this much fun!

Then tap *Ends*, and repeat the process to schedule the ending time. (The iPhone helpfully pre-sets the Ends time to one hour later.)

An *All-day* event, of course, means something that has no specific time of day associated with it: a holiday, a birthday, a book deadline. When you turn this option On, the Starts and Ends times disappear. Back on the calendar, the appointment jumps to the top of the list for that day.

Tip Calendar can handle multi-day appointments, too, like trips away. Turn on All-day—and then use the Starts and Ends controls to specify beginning and ending *dates*. On the iPhone, you'll see it as a list item that repeats on every day's square. Back on your computer, you'll see it as a banner stretching across the Month view.

Appointment, with times   *All-day event*

Tap Save when you're done.

- **Repeat.** The screen here contains common options for recurring events: every day, every week, and so on. It starts out saying None.

Once you've tapped a selection, you return to the Edit screen. Now you can tap the *End Repeat* button to specify when this event should *stop* repeating. If you leave the setting at *Repeat Forever*, you're stuck seeing this event repeating on your calendar until the end of time (a good choice for recording, say, your anniversary, especially if your spouse might be consulting the same calendar).

In other situations, you may prefer to spin the three dials (month, day, year) to specify an ending date, which is a useful option for car and mortgage payments.

- **Alert.** This screen tells Calendar how to notify you when a certain appointment is about to begin. Calendar can send any of four kinds of flags to get your attention. Tap how much notice you want: 5, 15, or 30 minutes before the big moment; an hour or two before; a day or two before; or on the day of the event.

When you tap Save and return to the main Add Event screen, you'll see that a new line, called *Second Alert*, has sprouted up beneath the first Alert line. This line lets you schedule a **second** warning for your appointment, which can occur either before or after the first one. Think of it as a backup alarm for events of extra urgency. Tap Save.

Once you've scheduled these alerts, at the appointed time(s), you'll see a message appear on the screen. (Even if the phone was asleep, it appears briefly.) You'll also hear a chirpy alarm sound.

 The iPhone doesn't play the sound if you turned off Calendar Alerts in Settings→Sounds. It also doesn't play if you silenced the phone with the silencer switch on the side.

- **Notes.** Here's your chance to customize your calendar event. You can type any text you want in the notes area—driving directions, contact phone numbers, a call history, or whatever. Tap Save when you're finished.

When you've completed filling in all these blanks, tap Done. Your newly scheduled event now shows up on the calendar.

 If you use iCal on the Macintosh, you might notice that the iPhone offers no way to place each new appointment into a *calendar*—that is, a color-coded category like Home or Social.

Instead, when you set up the iPhone for syncing, you can specify which iCal category *all* of the iPhone's newly created events fall into. See page 223 for details.

Editing, Rescheduling, and Deleting Events

To examine the details of an appointment in the calendar, tap it once. The Event screen appears, filled with the details you previously established.

To edit any of these characteristics, tap Edit. You return to what looks like a clone of the New Event screen shown on page 164.

Here, you can change the name, time, alarm, repeat schedule, or any other detail of the event, just the way you set them up to begin with.

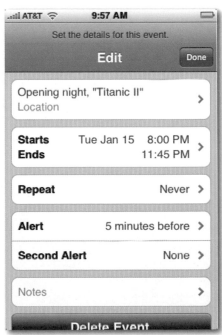

The one difference: This time, there's a big red Delete Event button at the bottom. That's the only way to erase an appointment from your calendar.

YouTube

YouTube, of course, is the stratospherically popular video-sharing Web site, where people post short videos of every description: funny clips from TV, homemade blooper reels, goofy short films, musical performances, bite-sized serial dramas, and so on. YouTube's fans watch 100 million little videos a day.

The YouTube application was the last one added to the iPhone. It wasn't even on the demo iPhone that Steve Jobs used when he unveiled the phone in January 2007. (In fact, when it finally was added in June, just before the iPhone went on sale, it merited an Apple press release all its own.)

Of course, you already have a Web browser on your iPhone—Safari. Why not just go to YouTube in the Web browser, the way millions of other people do?

Mainly because of Flash.

Long story: Most YouTube movies are in a format called Flash, which iPhone 1.0 doesn't recognize. Flash video, at least in YouTube's version, doesn't look so great, anyway. YouTube videos are famous for their blurry, mushy look.

So Apple approached YouTube and made a radical suggestion: Why not re-encode all of its millions of videos into H.264, a *much* higher quality format

that, coincidentally, is playable on the iPhone and the Apple TV?

Amazingly enough, YouTube agreed. (Chalk one up for Steve Jobs' reality distortion field.) At the launch of the iPhone, 10,000 YouTube videos had already been converted, with the rest planned for conversion by the fall of 2007.

So the YouTube app on the iPhone exists for two reasons. First, it makes accessing YouTube videos much easier than fumbling around at YouTube.com. Second, it saves you time because it displays only the high-quality H.264-formatted videos and hides the rest.

Finding a Video to Play

The YouTube program works much like the iPod program in that it's basically a collection of lists. Tap one of the icons at the bottom of the screen, for example, to find videos in any of these ways:

- **Featured.** A scrolling, flickable list of videos hand-picked by YouTube's editors. You get to see the name, length, star rating, and popularity (viewership) of each one

- **Most Viewed**. A popularity contest. Tap the buttons at the top to look over the most-viewed videos *Today*, *This Week*, or *All* (meaning "of all time"). Scroll to the bottom of the list and tap Load 25 More to see the next chunk of the list.

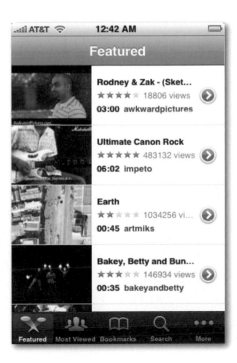

- **Bookmarks.** A list of videos you've flagged as your own personal faves, as described in a moment.

- **Search.** Makes the iPhone keyboard appear, so you can type a search phrase. YouTube produces a list of videos whose titles, descriptions, keywords, or creator names match what you typed.

If you tap More, you get three additional options:

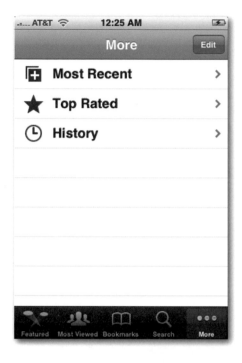

- **Most Recent.** These are the very latest videos that have been posted on YouTube.

- **Top Rated.** Whenever people watch a video on YouTube, they have the option of giving it a star rating. (You can't rate videos when you're viewing them on the iPhone.) This list rounds up the highest rated videos. Beware—you may be disappointed in the taste of the masses.

- **History.** This is a list of videos you've viewed recently on the iPhone—and a Clear button that nukes the list, so that people won't know what you've been watching.

Each of these lists offers a ⊙ button at the right side. Tap it to open the Details screen for that video, featuring a description, date, category, tags (keywords), uploader name, play length, number of views, links to related videos, and so on.

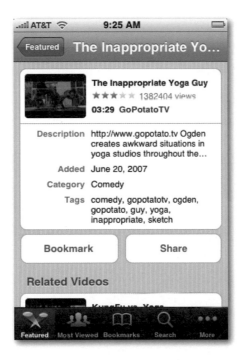

Also on this screen are two useful buttons: *Bookmark*, which adds this video to your own personal list of favorites (tap the Bookmarks button at the bottom of the screen to see that list), and *Share*, which switches into the Mail program and creates an outgoing message containing a link to that YouTube video. Address it and send along to anyone you think would be interested, thus fulfilling your duty as a cog in the great viral YouTube machine.

Playing YouTube Videos

To play a video, tap its row in any of the lists. Turn the iPhone 90 degrees counterclockwise—all videos play in horizontal orientation. The video begins playing automatically; you don't have to tap the ▶ button.

Here, you'll discover a basic truth about the YouTube app on the iPhone: Videos look **great** if you're connected to the Internet through a Wi-Fi hot spot. They look **not** so great if you're connected over AT&T's cellular EDGE network. When you're on EDGE, you get a completely different version of the video—smaller, coarser, and grainier. In fact, you may not be able to get videos to play at all over EDGE.

When you first start playing a video, you get the usual iPhone playback controls, like ▶▶|, |◀◀ ||, the volume slider, and the progress scrubber at the top. (See page 82 for details.) Here again, you can double-tap the screen to magnify the video slightly, just enough to eliminate the black bars on the sides of the screen (or tap the ⬉ button at the top-right corner to do the same).

The controls fade away after a moment, so they don't block your view. You can make them appear and disappear with a single tap on the video.

There are three icons on these controls, however, that **don't** also appear when you're playing iPod videos. First is the ⌓ button, which adds the video you're watching to your Bookmarks list, so you won't have to hunt around for it later.

Second is the ✉ button, which pauses the video and sends you to the Mail app, where a link to the video is pasted into an outgoing message for you.

Finally, there's a Done button at the top-left corner. It takes you out of the video you're watching and back to the list of YouTube videos.

Stocks

This one's for you, big-time day trader. The Stocks app tracks the rise and fall of the stocks in your portfolio. It connects to the Internet to download the very latest stock prices. (All right, maybe not the *very* latest. The price info may be delayed as much as 20 minutes, which is typical of free stock-info services.)

When you first fire it up, Stocks shows you a handful of sample high-tech stocks or, rather, their abbreviations. (They stand for the Dow Jones Industrial Index, Apple, Google, Yahoo, and AT&T, respectively.) Next to each, you see its current stock share price, and next to *that*, you see how much that price has gone up or down today. As a handy visual gauge to how much you should be elated or depressed, this final digit appears on a *green* background if it's gone up, or a *red* one if it's gone down.

Tap a stock name to view its stock-price graph at the bottom of the screen. You can even adjust the time scale of this graph by tapping the little interval buttons along the top edge: *1d* means "one day" (today); *1w* means "one week"; *1m*, *3m*, and *6m* refer to numbers of months; and *1y* and *2y* refer to years.

Finally, if you want more detailed information about a stock, tap its name and then tap the 💬! button in the lower-left corner. The iPhone fires up its Web browser and takes you to the Yahoo Finance page for that particular stock, showing the company's Web site, more detailed stock information, and even recent news articles that may have affected the stock's price.

Customizing Your Portfolio

It's fairly unlikely that *your* stock portfolio contains Apple, Google, Yahoo, and AT&T (although you'd be rich if it did). Fortunately, you can customize the list of stocks to reflect the companies you *do* own (or that you want to track without owning).

To edit the list, tap the ❸ button in the lower-right corner. You arrive at the editing screen, where you can:

- **Delete a stock** by tapping the ⊖ button and then the Delete confirmation button.

- **Add a stock** by tapping the **+** button at the top-left corner; the Add Stock screen and the keyboard appear. The idea here is that you're not expected to know every company's stock-symbol abbreviation. So type in the company's *name*, and then tap Search. The iPhone then shows you, just above the keyboard, a scrolling list of companies with matching names. Tap the one you want to track. You return to the stocks-list editing screen.

- **Choose % or Numbers.** You can specify how you want to see the changes in stock prices in the far-right column: either as *numbers* ("+2.23") or as *percentages* ("+ 0.65%"). Tap the corresponding button at the bottom of this screen.

When you're finished setting up your stock list, tap Done.

Maps

It's awfully nice that Google's CEO is on the board of Apple. It means that these two tech giants can collaborate in cool new ways—and Google Maps on the iPhone is one of them. It's *wicked* useful.

Google Maps on the Web is awesome enough. It lets you type in any address or point of interest in the U.S. or many other countries—and see it plotted on a map. You have a choice of a street-map diagram or an actual aerial photo, taken by satellite. Google Maps is an incredible resource for planning a drive, scoping out a new city before you travel there, investigating the proximity of a new house to schools and stores, seeing how far a hotel is from the beach, or just generally blowing your mind with a new view of the world.

And now you've got Google Maps on the iPhone, with even more features—like turn-by-turn driving directions, live national Yellow Pages business directory, and real-time traffic-jam alerts, represented by color coding on the roads of the map.

 Note Your happiness with Maps depends a lot on how you're connected to the Internet. A Wi-Fi connection is fairly snappy. A cellular EDGE connection may mean waiting a few seconds every time you scroll or zoom the map.

Browsing the Maps

The very first time you open Maps, you see a miniature U.S. map. Double-tap to zoom in on a region of the country; double-tap again to zoom in on a state; and so on, until you're seeing actual city blocks. You can also pinch or spread

two fingers (page 18) to magnify or shrink the view. Drag or flick to scroll around the map.

To zoom *out* again, you use a technique that's not available anywhere else on the iPhone: the *two-finger tap.* So—zoom in with *two* taps, one finger; zoom out with *one* tap, two fingers.

At any time, you can tap the Satellite button below the screen to view the same region as an aerial photo. (There's no guarantee it's a very *recent* photo—different parts of the Google Maps database use photography taken at different times—but it's still very cool.)

 If you zoom in far enough, the satellite photo eventually vanishes; you see only a tiled message that says, "No Image" over and over again. In other words, you've reached the resolution limits of Google's satellite imagery. Do some two-finger taps to back out again.

Searching the Maps

Instead of tapping your way to a particular spot on the map, it's often far more efficient to *type* a location, especially when you don't know where that location is to begin with.

Tap in the Search box to summon the iPhone keyboard. (If there's already something in the Search box, tap the button to clear it out.)

Here's what Maps can find for you:

- **An address.** You can skip the periods (and usually the commas, too). You can use abbreviations, too. Typing *710 w end ave ny ny* will find 710 West End Avenue, New York, New York.

  Tip: You can type a Zip code instead of the city and state in any of these examples.

- **An intersection.** Type *57th and lexington, ny ny*. Maps will find the spot where East 57th Street crosses Lexington Avenue in New York City.

- **A city.** Type *chicago il* to see a map of the city. You can zoom in from there.

- **A Zip code.** Type *10024* to see that region.

- **A point of interest.** Type *washington monument* or *niagara falls*.

When Maps finds a specific address, an animated, red-topped pushpin comes flying down onto its precise spot on the map. A translucent bubble identifies the location by name.

> **Tip** Tap the bubble to hide it. Tap the pushpin to bring the bubble back.

Finding Friends and Businesses

Maps is also plugged into your Contacts list, which makes it especially easy to find a friend's house (or just see how ritzy his neighborhood is).

Instead of typing an address into the Search bar, tap the button at the right end of it. You arrive at the Bookmarks/Recents/Contacts screen, containing three lists that can save you a lot of typing.

Two of them are described in the next section. But if you tap Contacts, you see your master address book (Chapter 2). Tap the name of someone you want to find. In a flash, Maps drops a red animated pushpin onto the map to identify that address.

> **Tip** If you're handy with the iPhone keyboard, you can save a few taps. Type part of a person's name into the Search bar. As you go, the iPhone displays a list of matching names. Tap the one you want to find on the map.

That pushpin business also comes into play when you use Maps as a glorified national Yellow Pages. If you type, for example, *pizza austin tx* or *pharmacy 60609*, those red pushpins show you all of the drugstores in that Chicago Zip code. It's a great way to find a gas station, cash machine, or hospital in a pinch. Tap a pushpin to see the name of the corresponding business.

You can tap the ⊘ button in the pushpin's label bubble to open a details screen about the pushpin address. If you've searched for a friend, you see the corresponding Contacts card. If you've searched for a business, you get a screen containing its phone number, address, Web site, and so on. Remember that you can tap a Web address to open it, or tap the phone number to dial it. ("Hello, what time do you close today?")

Tip If the cluster of pushpins makes it hard to see what you're doing, tap List. You see a neat text list of the same businesses. Tap one to see it alone on the map, or tap ⊘ to see its details card.

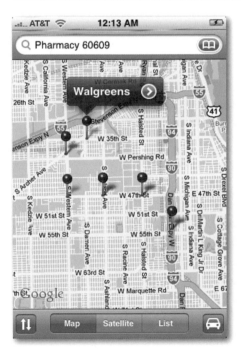

In both cases, you get two useful buttons, labeled *Directions To Here* and *Directions From Here*. See page 181 for details.

You also get an *Add to Bookmarks* button, which saves this address for instant recall later, as described next.

Bookmarks and Recents

Let's face it, the iPhone's tiny keyboard can be a little fussy. One nice thing about Maps is the way it tries to eliminate typing at every step.

If you tap the 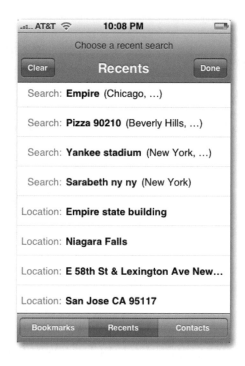 button at the right end of the Search bar, for example, you get the Bookmarks/Recents/Contacts screen—three lists that spare you from having to type stuff.

- **Bookmarks** are addresses that you've flagged for later use by tapping Add to Bookmarks, as described on the previous page.

  For sure, you should bookmark your own home and workplace. Those bookmarks will make it much easier to request driving directions, as described in the next section.

- **Recents** are searches you've conducted. You'd be surprised at how often you want to call up the same spot again later—and now you can, just by tapping its name in this list. You can also tap Clear to empty the list (if, for example, you intend to elope and don't want your parents to find out what you've been planning).

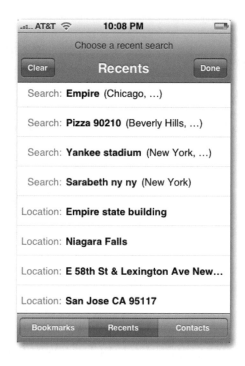

- **Contacts** is your iPhone address book, as described earlier. One tap maps out where someone lives.

Driving Directions

If you tap the 🔃 button (lower-left corner), the Search bar turns into *two* Search bars: one labeled *Start* and the other *End*. Plug in two addresses and let Google Maps guide you from the first to the second.

The iPhone doesn't have a GPS receiver, so it doesn't actually know where you are. It's not one of those boxes you put on your dashboard where the nice robot lady says, "In three-tenths of a mile, turn right onto I-95." But as you'll see in a moment, it's a pretty good fake version of that.

Begin by filling in the Start and End boxes. You can use any of the address shortcuts described on page 178, or you can tap the 📖 button to specify a bookmark, a recent search, or a name in Contacts. (Or, after performing any search that produces a pushpin, you can tap the ⊙ button in the pushpin's label bubble, and then tap *Directions To Here* or *Direction From Here* on the details screen.)

Then tap Route. In just a moment, Maps displays an overview of the route you're about to drive. At the top of the screen, you see the total distance and the amount of time it'll take (if you stay within the speed limit).

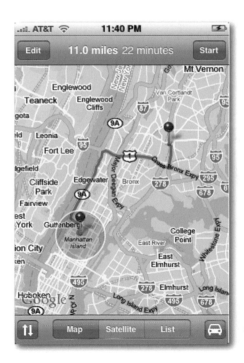
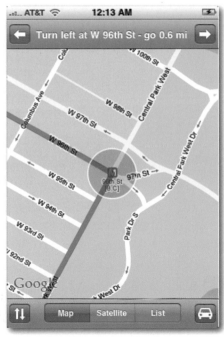

Tap Start to see the first driving instruction. The map also zooms in to the actual road you'll be traveling, which looks like it's been drawn in with purple highlighter. It's just like having a printout from MapQuest—the directions at the top of the screen say, for example, "Head east on Canterbury Ln toward Blackbird Ave – go .5 mi." Unlike MapQuest, though, you see only one instruction at a time (the current step), and you don't have to clutch and peer at a crumpled piece of paper while you're driving.

Tap the ← or → buttons to see the previous or next driving instruction. At any time, you can also tap List at the bottom of the screen to see the master list of turns. Tap an instruction to see a closeup of that turn on the map.

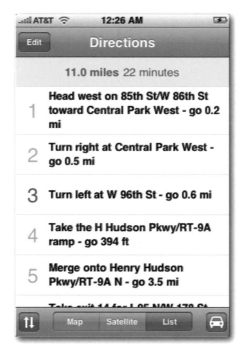

To adjust one of the addresses, tap the current driving instruction; the Search boxes reappear. And to exit the driving-instruction mode, tap the ⇅ button again.

 Tip If you tap the ⇅ button, you swap the Start and End points. That's a great way to find your way back after your trip.

Traffic

No, the iPhone doesn't have real GPS, but how's this for a consolation prize? Free, real-time traffic reporting—the same information you'd have to pay XM Satellite Radio $10 a month for.

Just tap the  button (lower-right corner). Now you'll see stretches of road change color to indicate how bad the traffic is.

- **Green** means the traffic is moving at least at 50 miles an hour.

- **Yellow** indicate speeds from 25 to 50 m.p.h.

- **Red** means that the road is like a parking lot. The traffic's moving under 25 m.p.h. Time to tap Home→iPod and entertain yourself.

If you don't see any color coding, it's because Google doesn't have any information for those roads. Usually, the color-coding appears only on highways, and only in metropolitan areas.

Weather

This little widget shows a handy current-conditions display for your city (or any other city), and, at your option, even offers a six-day forecast.

Before you get started, the most important step is to click the ❶ button at the lower-right corner. The widget flips around.

On the back panel, you can delete the sample city (Cupertino, California, which is Apple's headquarters) by tapping ⊖ and then Delete. And you can add your own city, or cities of interest, by tapping ✚. The Add Location screen and keyboard appear, so you can type your city and state or zip code.

When you tap Search, you're shown a list of matching cities; tap the one whose weather you want to track.

When you return to the configuration screen, you can also specify whether you prefer degrees Celsius or degrees Fahrenheit. Click Done.

Now the front of the widget displays the name of your town, today's predicted high and low, the current temperature, a six-day forecast, and a graphic representation of the sky conditions (sunny, cloudy, rainy, and so on).

There's nothing to tap here except the ☻! icon at lower-left. It fires up the Safari browser, which loads itself with Yahoo's information page about that city. Depending on the city, you might see a City Guide, city news, city photos, and more.

If you've added more than one city to the list, by the way, just flick your finger right or left to shuffle through the Weather screens for the different cities on your list. The tiny row of bullets beneath the display correspond to the number of Weather cities you've set up—and the white bold one indicates where you are in the sequence.

Clock

It's not just a clock—it's more like a time factory. Hiding behind this single icon on the Home screen are four programs: a world clock, an alarm clock, a stopwatch, and a countdown timer.

World Clock

When you tap World Clock at the bottom of the Clock screen, you start out with only one clock, showing the current time in Apple's own Cupertino, California.

Sure, this clock shows the current time, but your phone's status bar does that. The neat part is that you can open up *several* of these clocks, and set each one up to show the time in a different city. The result looks like the row of clocks in a hotel lobby, making you look Swiss and precise.

By checking these clocks, you'll know what time it is in some remote city, so you don't wind up waking somebody up at what turns out to be three in the morning.

To specify which city's time appears on the clock, tap the **+** button at the upper-right corner. The keyboard pops up so you can type the name of a

major city. As you type, a scrolling list of matching city names appears above the keyboard; tap the one whose time you want to track.

As soon as you tap a city name, you return to the World Clock display. The color of the clock indicates whether it's daytime (white) or night (black). Note, too, that you can scroll the list of clocks. You're not limited to four, although only four fit the screen at once.

To edit the list of clocks, tap Edit. Now you can delete a city clock by tapping ⊖ and then Delete, or drag clocks up or down in the list using the ☰ grip strip as a handle. Then tap Done.

Alarm

If you travel much, this feature could turn out to be one of your iPhone's most useful functions. It's reliable, it's programmable, and it even wakes up *the phone* first, if necessary, to wake *you*.

To set an alarm, tap Alarm at the bottom of the Clock program's screen. Tap the **+** button at the upper-right corner to open the Add Alarm screen.

Your options here are:

- **Repeat.** Tap to specify what days this alarm rings. You can specify, for example, Mondays, Wednesdays, and Fridays by tapping those three buttons. (Tap a day-of-week button again to turn off its checkmark.) Tap Back when you're done.

- **Sound.** Here's where you specify what sound you want to ring when the time comes. You can choose from any of the iPhone's 25 ringtone sounds. Tap Back.

Tip Alarm, Crickets, Digital, and Old Phone are the longest and highest sounds. They're the ones most likely to get your attention.

- **Snooze.** If this option is on, then at the appointed time, the alarm message on the screen offers you a Snooze button. Tap it for ten more minutes of blissful sleep, at which point the iPhone tries again to get your attention.

- **Label.** Tap to give this alarm a description, like "Get dressed for wedding." That message appears on the screen when the alarm goes off.

- **Time dials.** Spin these three vertical wheels—hour, minute, AM/PM—to specify the time you want the alarm to go off.

When you finally tap Save, you return to the Alarm screen, which lists your new alarm. Just tap the On/Off switch to cancel an alarm. It stays in the list, though, so you can quickly reactivate it another day, without having to redo the whole thing. You can tap the ✚ button to set another alarm, if you like.

Note, too that the ◑ icon appears in the status bar at the top of the iPhone screen. That's your indicator that the alarm is set.

To delete or edit an alarm, tap Edit. Tap ⊖ and then Delete to get rid of an alarm completely, or tap the alarm's name to return to the setup screen, where you can make changes to the time, name, sound, and so on.

So what happens when the alarm goes off? The iPhone wakes itself up, if it was asleep. A message appears on the screen, identifying the alarm and the time.

And, of course, the sound rings. This alarm is the one and only iPhone sound that you'll hear *even if the silencer switch is turned on*. Apple figures that if you've gone to the trouble of setting an alarm, you probably *really* want to know about it, even if you forgot to turn the ringer back on.

In that case, the screen says, "slide to stop alarm."

To cut the ringing short, tap OK or Snooze. After the alarm plays (or you cut it short), its On/Off switch goes to Off (on the Alarms screen).

 Tip With some planning, you can also give yourself a silent, *vibrating* alarm. It can be a subtle cue that it's time to wrap up your speech, conclude a meeting, or end a date so you can get home to watch *Lost*.

You have to set this up right, though. If you just turn on the iPhone's ring silencer (page 12), then the phone won't ring *or* vibrate. If you choose None as the alarm sound, it won't ring or vibrate, either. And, of course, you have to make sure the Vibrate mode is turned on in Settings→Sounds.

Here's the trick, then: *Do* choose an alarm sound. And *don't* turn off your ringer. Instead, use the volume keys to crank the iPhone's volume all the way to zero. Now, the phone vibrates at the appointed time—but it won't make a sound.

Stopwatch

You've never met a more beautiful stopwatch than this one.

Tap Start to begin timing something: a runner, a public speaker, a train, a long-winded person who's arguing with you.

While the digits are flying by, you can tap Lap as often as you like. Each time, the list in the bottom part of the screen identifies how much time had elapsed at the moment you hit Lap. It's a way for you to compare, for example, how much time a runner is spending on each lap around a track.

 Note On most stopwatches, of course, the *grand total* time keeps ticking away in the main display. The fact that the iPhone's main counter resets to zero each time you tap Lap appears to be a bug in the 1.0 software.

You can do other things on the iPhone while the stopwatch is counting, by the way. In fact, the timer keeps ticking away even when the iPhone is asleep! As a result, you can time long-term events, like how long it takes an ice sculpture to melt, the time it takes for a bean seed to sprout, or the length of a Michael Bay movie.

Tap Stop to freeze the counter; tap Start to resume the timing. If you tap Reset, you reset the counter to zero and erase all the lap times.

Timer

The fourth Clock mini-app is a countdown timer. You input a starting time, and it counts down to zero.

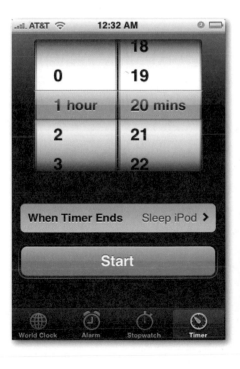

Countdown timers are everywhere in life. They measure the time of periods in sports games, of cooking times in the kitchen, of stunts on *Survivor*. But on the iPhone, the timer has a especially handy function: It can turn off the music or video after a specified amount of time. In short, it's a Sleep timer that plays you to sleep, then shuts off to save power.

To set the timer, open the Clock app and then tap Timer. Spin the two dials to specify the number of hours and minutes you want to count down.

Then tap the When Timer Ends control to set up what happens when the timer reaches 0:00. Most of the options here are ringtone sounds, so you'll have an audible cue that the time's up. The top one, though, Sleep iPod, is the aforementioned Sleep timer. It stops audio and video playback at the appointed time, so that you (and the iPhone) can go to sleep. Tap Set.

Finally, tap Start. Big clock digits count down toward zero. While it's in progress, you can do other things on the iPhone, change the When Timer Ends settings, or just hit Cancel to forget the whole thing.

Calculator

The iPhone wouldn't be much of a computer without a calculator, now would it?

And here it is, your basic four-function memory calculator. Tap out equations (like *15.4 x 300=*) to see the answer at the top.

> **Tip** When you tap one of the operators (like x, +, –, or ÷) it sprouts a white outline to help you remember which operation is in progress. Let's see an ordinary calculator do *that!*

The Memory function works like a short-term storage area that retains numbers temporarily, making it easier to work on complicated problems.

When you press *m+*, whatever number is on the screen gets added to the number already in the memory and the *mr/mc* button glows with a white ring to let you know you've stored something there. Press *m–* to *subtract* the currently displayed number from the number in memory.

And what *is* the number in memory? Press *mr/mc* to display it—to use it in a subsequent calculation, for example.

Finally, tap *mr/mc* twice to clear the memory and do away with the white ring.

Notes

The Notes app is the iPhone's answer to a word processor. It's simple in the extreme—there's no formatting, for example, and no way to sync your notes back to the computer. Still, it's nice to be able to jot down lists, reminders, and brainstorms. (You can then email them to yourself when you're finished.)

The first time you open Notes, you see what looks like a yellow lined legal pad. Tap on the lines to make the keyboard appear so you can begin typing. (See page 21 for tips on using the keyboard and the editing loupe.)

When you're finished with a note for now, tap Done. The keyboard goes away, and a ✚ button appears at the top right. That button lets you open a new note.

As you create more pages, the Notes button (top left) becomes more useful. It's your table of contents for the Notes pad. It displays the first line of typing in each note page you've created, along with the time or date you created it. (The **+** button appears here, too.) To open a note, tap its name.

Whenever you've put away the keyboard by tapping Done, by the way, a handy row of icons appears at the bottom of your Notes page. They're pretty self-explanatory, but here's the rundown:

- ←, →. These buttons let you skip to the previous or next page without requiring a detour to the master Notes list.

- ✉. Tap to send your note by email to someone. (A handy way to get an important note back to your own home computer.) The iPhone fires up its Mail program, creates a new outgoing message, pastes the first line of the note into the Subject line, and then pastes the Notes text into the body. All you have to do is address the note, edit the body if necessary, and hit Send. Afterward, the iPhone politely returns you to the note you were editing.

- 🗑. Tap to delete the current note. After you confirm your decision, the Trash can's lid opens, the note folds itself up and flies in, and then the lid closes up again. Cute—real cute.

10 iTunes for iPhoners

F or the five or six people out there who've never heard of it, iTunes is Apple's multimedia, multifunction jukebox software. It's been loading music onto iPods since the turn of the 21st century. And without it, you won't get very far with your iPhone.

That's because the iTunes program is your iPhone's loading dock, administrative department, media supplier, and best friend. Most people use iTunes to manipulate their digital movies, photos, and music, from converting songs off a CD into iPhone-ready music files to buying songs, audio books and video online. But you, as an iPhone owner, need it even more urgently, because you can't activate your iPhone or sign up for AT&T service without it.

If you already have a copy of iTunes on your Mac or PC, you may have encountered a warning that iTunes wants to update itself to at least version 7.3. With a click on the OK button, you can download and install that version. And you should—your iPhone won't work with earlier versions.

If you've never had *any* version of iTunes, fire up your Web browser and go to *www.apple.com/itunes/download.*

Once the file lands on your computer, double-click the installer icon and follow the instructions onscreen to add iTunes to your life. This chapter give you a crash course in iTunes. The next chapter covers syncing it with your iPhone.

The iTunes Window: What's Where

Here's a quick tour of the main iTunes window and what all its parts do.

The Source panel at the left side lists all the audio and video sources you can tap into at the moment. Clicking a name in the Source list makes the main song-list area change accordingly, like so:

Source list

- **Library.** Click this icon to see the contents of all your different media collections. As you add movies, games, music, podcasts, and other stuff to iTunes, subheadings appear (Music, TV Shows, Podcasts, and so on) under the Library heading. Click one to see what audio and video your computer has in that category.

- **Store.** Click the icons to shop for new stuff in the iTunes Store (music, movies, TV shows, free podcasts) or see the list of things you've already bought.

- **CD.** If there's a CD in the computer's drive, it shows up in the Devices areas of the Source list. Click it to see, and play, the songs on it.

- **iPhone.** When it's connected and sitting in its sync cradle, an icon for your iPhone shows up here, too, so you can see what's on it.

- **Shared**. This list lets you browse the music libraries of *other* iTunes addicts on your network and play their music on your own computer. (Yes, it's legal.)

- **Playlists**. *Playlists* are lists of songs that you assemble yourself, mixing and matching music from different CDs and other sources as you see fit (page 202). Here's where you see them listed.

Here's the basic rule of using iTunes: Click one of these headings in the Source list to reveal what's *in* that source. The contents appear in the center part of the iTunes window.

The playback and volume controls, which work just as they do on the iPhone, are in the top left corner of iTunes. At the upper-right corner is a Search box that lets you pluck one track out of a haystack. Next to it, you'll find handy buttons to change views within the window. (Cover Flow, like on the iPhone, is the third button in this grouping.)

Five Ways to Get Music

Once you have iTunes, the next step is to start filling it with music and video so you can get all that goodness onto your iPhone. iTunes gives you at least five options right off the bat.

Let iTunes Find Your Existing Songs

If you've had a computer for longer than a few days, you probably already have some songs in the popular MP3 format on your hard drive, perhaps from a file-sharing service or free music Web site. If so, the first time you open iTunes, it offers to search your PC or Mac for music and add it to its library. Click Yes; iTunes goes hunting around your hard drive.

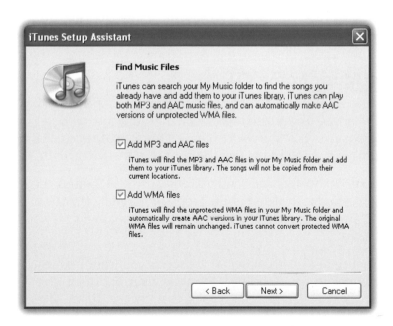

The iTunes Store

Another way to get some music and movies for iPhone and iTunes is to buy them in the iTunes Store.

Click the iTunes Store icon in the list on the left side of the iTunes window. Once you land on the Store's main page and set up your iTunes account (page 264), you can buy and download songs, audio books, and videos. This material goes straight into your iTunes library, just a short sync away from the iPhone.

Import Music from a CD

iTunes can also convert tracks from audio CDs into iPhone-ready digital music files. Just start up iTunes, and then stick a CD into your computer's CD drive. The program asks you if you want to convert the songs to audio files for iTunes. (If it doesn't ask, click Import CD at the bottom of the window.)

Once you tell it to import the music, iTunes walks you through the process. If you're connected to the Internet, the program automatically downloads song titles and artist information for the CD and begins to add the songs to the iTunes library.

If you want time to think about which songs you want from each CD, you can tell iTunes to download only the song *titles*, and then give you a few minutes to ponder your selections. To do that, choose iTunes→Preferences→ Advanced→Importing (Mac) or Edit→Preferences→Advanced→Importing (Windows). Use the "On CD Insert:" pop-up menu to choose "Show CD."

From now on, if you don't want the entire album, you can exclude the dud songs by turning off their checkmarks. Then click Import CD in the bottom-right corner of the screen.

 Tip You can ⌘-click (Mac) or Ctrl+click (Windows) any box to turn *all* the checkboxes on or off. This technique is ideal when you want only one or two songs in the list. First, turn all checkboxes off, and then turn those *two* back on again.

In that same Preferences box, you can also choose the *format* (the file type) and *bit rate* (the amount of audio data compressed into that format) for your imported tracks. The factory setting is the AAC format at 128 kilobits per second.

Most people think these settings make for fine-sounding music files, but you can change your settings to, for example, MP3, which is another format that lets you cram big music into small space. Upping the bit rate from 128 kbps to 256 kbps makes for richer sounding music files—that also happen to take up more room because the files are bigger (and space is at a premium on the iPhone). The choice is yours.

As the import process starts, iTunes moves down the list of checked songs, ripping each one to a file in your Home→Music→iTunes→iTunes Music folder (Mac) or My Documents→My Music→iTunes→iTunes Music (Windows). An orange squiggle next to a song name means the track is currently converting. Feel free to switch into other programs, answer email, surf the Web, and do other work while the ripping is under way.

Once the importing is finished, each imported song bears a green checkmark, and iTunes signals its success with a melodious flourish. Now you have some brand-new files in your iTunes library.

Tip If you always want *all* the songs on that stack of CDs next to your computer, change the iTunes CD import preferences to "Import CD and Eject" to save yourself some clicking. When you insert a CD, iTunes imports it and spits it out, ready for the next one.

Podcasts

The iTunes Store houses thousands upon thousands of podcasts, those free audio (and video!) recordings put out by everyone from big TV networks to a guy in his barn with a microphone.

To explore podcasts, click Podcasts on the Store's main page. Now you can browse shows by category, search for podcast names by keyword, or click around until you find something that sounds good.

Many podcasters produce regular installments of their shows, releasing new episodes onto the Internet when they're ready. You can have iTunes keep a look out for fresh editions of your favorite podcasts and automatically download them for you, where you can find them in the Podcasts area in the iTunes source list. All you have to do is *subscribe* to the podcast, which takes a couple of clicks in the Store.

If you want to try out a podcast, click the Get Episode link near its title to download just that one show. If you like it (or know that you're going to like it before you even download the first episode), there's also a Subscribe button at the top of the page that signs you up to receive all future episodes.

You play a podcast just like any other file in iTunes: Double-click the file name in the iTunes window and use the playback controls in the upper-left corner. On the iPhone, podcasts show up in their own list.

Audiobooks

Some people like the sound of a good book, and iTunes has plenty to offer in its Audiobooks area. You can find verbal versions of the latest bestsellers here in the store; prices depend on the title, but are usually cheaper than buying a hardback copy of the book—which would be four times the size of your iPhone anyway.

If iTunes doesn't offer the audiobook you're interested in, you can find a larger sample (over 35,000 of them) at Audible.com. This Web store sells all kinds of audio books, recorded periodicals like *The New York Times*, and radio shows.

To purchase Audible's wares, though, you need to go to the Web site and create an Audible account.

If you use Windows, you can download from Audible.com a little program called AudibleManager, which catapults your Audible downloads into iTunes for you. On the Mac, Audible files land in iTunes automatically when you buy them.

And when those files do land in iTunes, you can play them on your computer or send them over to the iPhone with a quick sync.

Playlists

A *playlist* is a list of songs that you've decided should go together. It can be any group of songs arranged in any order, all according to your whims. For example, if you're having a party, you can make a playlist from the current Top 40 and dance music in your music library. Some people may question your taste if you, say, alternate tracks from *La Bohème* with Queen's *A Night at the Opera*, but hey—it's your playlist.

Playlists are especially important in the new world of iPhone, because they're the basic unit of music-loading. If you have a regular iPod, you can drag individual songs onto its icon in iTunes, but the iPhone is different. You can put music onto the iPhone *only* if they're in playlists.

To create a playlist, press ⌘-N (Mac) or Ctrl+N (Windows). Or choose File→New Playlist, or click the ✚ button below the Source list.

All freshly minted playlists start out with the impersonal name "Untitled Playlist." Fortunately, the renaming rectangle is open and highlighted. Just type a better name: *Cardio Workout*, *Shoe-Shopping Tunes*, *Hits of the Highland Lute*, or whatever you want to call it. As you add them, your playlists alphabetize themselves in the Source window.

File	Edit	Controls	View	Store	Advanced
New Playlist					Ctrl+N
New Playlist from Selection					
New Smart Playlist...					Ctrl+Alt+N
New Folder					Ctrl+Shift+N
Add File to Library...					Ctrl+O
Add Folder to Library...					
Close Window					Ctrl+W
Import...					Ctrl+Shift+O
Export...					
Export Library...					
Back Up to Disc...					
Get Info					Ctrl+I
My Rating					
Edit Smart Playlist					
Show in Windows Explorer					Ctrl+R
Show Current Song					Ctrl+L

Once you've created this spanking new playlist, you're ready to add your songs or videos. The quickest way is to drag their names directly onto the playlist's icon.

> **Tip** Instead of making an empty playlist and then dragging songs into it, you can work the other way. You can scroll through a big list of songs, selecting tracks as you go by ⌘-clicking on the Mac or Ctrl+clicking in Windows—and then, when you're finished, choose File→New Playlist From Selection. All the songs you selected immediately appear on a brand new playlist.

When you drag a song title onto a playlist, you're not making a copy of the song. In essence, you're creating an *alias* or *shortcut* of the original, which means you can have the same song on several different playlists.

That nice iTunes even gives you some playlists of its own devising, like "Top 25 Most Played" and "Purchased" (a convenient place to find all your iTunes Store goodies listed in one place).

Editing and Deleting Playlists

A playlist is easy to change. With just a little light mousework, you can:

- **Change the order of songs on the playlist.** Click at the top of the first column in the playlist window (the one with the numbers next to the songs) and drag song titles up or down within the playlist window to reorder them.

- **Add new songs to the playlist.** Tiptoe through your iTunes library and drag more songs into a playlist.

- **Delete songs from the playlist.** If your playlist needs pruning, or that banjo tune just doesn't fit in with the brass-band tracks, you can ditch it quickly: Click the song in the playlist window and hit Delete or Backspace to get rid of it. When iTunes asks you to confirm your decision, click Yes.

Remember, deleting a song from a playlist doesn't delete it from your music library—it just removes the title from your *playlist*. (Only pressing Delete or Backspace when the Library Music icon is selected gets rid of the song for good.)

- **Delete the whole playlist.** To delete an entire playlist, click it in the Source list and press Delete (Backspace). Again, this zaps only the playlist itself, not all the stored songs you had in it. (Those are still in your computer's iTunes folder.)

 Tip If you want to see how many playlists a certain song appears on, select the track, ⌘-click (Mac) or Ctrl+click (Windows), and choose "Show in Playlist" in the pop-up menu.

Authorizing Computers

When you create the account in iTunes (a requirement for having an iPhone; see page 264), you automatically *authorize* that computer to play purchases from the iTunes Store. Authorization is Apple's way of making sure you don't go playing those music tracks on more than five computers, which would greatly displease the record companies.

You can copy your purchases onto a maximum of four other computers. To authorize each one to play music from your account, choose Store→Authorize Computer. (Don't worry, you just have to do this once per machine.)

When you've maxed out your limit and can't authorize any more computers, you need to *deauthorize* one. On the computer you wish to demote, choose Store→Deauthorize Computer.

> **Note** Not all songs you buy from iTunes are copy-protected. The ones labeled as iTunes Plus songs cost 30 cents more than regular songs ($1.30 total) and have slightly higher audio quality—and they're *not* copy-protected. You can play them on any player that recognizes AAC files.
>
> Then again, you can't go nuts, uploading them all over the Internet. Your name and email address are embedded in the file and quite visible to anyone (including any Apple lawyer) who chooses the track, chooses File→Get Info, and clicks the Summary tab.

Geeks' Nook: File Formats

It's a chronic headache in the modern age: There are just too many file formats for digital audio and video. Only Apple players play the songs you buy from iTunes. Conversely, you can't play the copy-protected songs from any other music store on an iPod or iPhone.

So what, exactly, *can* the iPhone play? Anything iTunes can play.

Which means:

- **Video formats** like H.264 and MPEG-4 (files whose names end with .m4v, .mp4, and .mov).

- **Audio formats** like MP3, AAC, protected AAC (that is, iTunes Store songs), MP3, Audible (formats 1, 2, and 3), Apple Lossless, AIFF, and WAV.

> **Tip** A free software program called Handbrake (*http://handbrake.m0k.org/*), available for Macintosh or Windows, can convert DVD movies into the .mp4 files that can play on your iPhone. And a $30 Apple program called QuickTime Player Pro, also for Mac and Windows, can convert dozens of other formats into iTunes/iPhone-compatible ones.

11 Syncing the iPhone

When you get right down to it, the iPhone is pretty much the same idea as a PalmPilot: it's a pocket-sized data bucket that lets you carry around the most useful subset of the information on your Mac or PC. In the iPhone's case, that's music, photos, movies, calendar, address book, email settings, and Web bookmarks.

Transferring data between the iPhone and the computer is called *synchronization*, or syncing. Syncing is sometimes a one-way street, and sometimes it's bidirectional:

- **Contacts, calendars, and Web bookmarks** get copied in both directions. After a sync, your computer and your phone contain exactly the same information. So if you enter an appointment on the iPhone, it gets copied to your computer—and vice versa. If you edit the *same* contact or appointment on both machines at once, your computer asks you which one "wins."

- **Audio files, video files, photos on your computer, and email-account information** go only one way: Computer→iPhone.

- **Photos you take with the iPhone's camera** get copied the other way: iPhone→computer.

This chapter covers the ins and outs—or, rather, backs and forths—of iPhone syncing.

Automatic Syncing

So how do you sync? You put the iPhone into its cradle. That's it. As long as the cradle is plugged into your computer's USB port, iTunes opens automatically and the synchronization begins. iTunes controls all iPhone synchronization, acing as a the software bridge between phone and computer.

Your photo-editing program (like iPhoto or Photoshop Elements) probably springs open every time you connect the iPhone, too. See page 215 for the solution.

When the iPhone and the computer are communicating, the iTunes window and the iPhone screen both say "Sync in progress."

Unlike an iPod, which gets very angry (and can potentially scramble your data) if you interrupt while its "Do not disconnect" screen is up, the iPhone is much more understanding about interruptions. If you need to use the iPhone for a moment, just drag your finger across the "slide to cancel" slider on the screen. The sync pauses. When you put the phone back in the cradle, the sync intelligently resumes.

In fact, if someone dares to call you while you're in mid-sync, the iPhone cancels the session *itself* so you can pick up the call. Just reconnect it to the computer when you're done chatting so it can finish syncing.

 Apple says that a USB 2.0 connection is required for iPhone syncing, but that's not really true. You can sync on an old USB 1 computer, too. You'll just wait a lot longer.

Manual Syncing, Four Ways

But what if you don't *want* iTunes to fire up and start syncing every time you connect your iPhone? What if, for example, you want to change the assortment of music and video that's about to get copied to it? Or what if you just don't like matters being taken out of your hands, because it reminds you too much of robot overlords?

In that case, you can stop the autosyncing in four different ways:

- **Stop iTunes from syncing the iPhone just this time.** As you put the iPhone in its cradle, hold down the Shift+Control keys (Windows) or the ⌘-Option keys (Mac) until the iPhone pops up in the iTunes window. Now you can see what's on the iPhone and change what will be synced to it—but no syncing takes place until you command it.

- **Stop iTunes from syncing automatically when you plug in the iPhone.** Connect the two, click the iPhone icon, click the Summary tab, and turn off "Automatically sync when this iPhone is connected." iTunes will no longer open automatically when you connect the phone (and therefore it won't sync).

- **Stop iTunes from autosyncing any iPhone, ever.** In iTunes, choose Edit→Preferences (Windows) or iTunes→Preferences (Mac). Click the iPhone tab and turn on "Disable automatic syncing for all iPhones." This setting overrides the "Automatically sync" setting on the Summary screen when the iPhone is connected.

- **Sync the iPhone manually.** With the iPhone in the cradle, specify what you want copied to it (using the various tabs in iTunes, as described next); click the Summary tab; and then click Apply. (The button says Sync instead if you haven't changed any settings.)

Click Apply to enforce any changes you make in the syncing preferences.

Note An iPod has a setting that lets you manage your audio and video files manually, by *dragging* them onto the iPod icon in the iTunes source list. The iPhone, however, is fussier, and wont let you drag and drop files onto it. You must use the various sync tabs described in the following pages.

What's On Your iPhone?

Once your iPhone is seated in the sync cradle, click its icon in the iTunes source list. The middle part of the iTunes window now reveals six file-folder tabs, representing the six categories of stuff you can sync to your iPhone. Here's what each one tells you:

- **Summary.** This screen gives basic stats on your iPhone, like its serial number, capacity, and phone number. Buttons in the middle let you check for iPhone software updates or restore it to its out-of-the-box state (page 271). At the bottom of the screen, you can specify *how* and *what* you'd like to sync.

- **Info.** The settings here control the syncing of your contacts, calendars, email account settings, and bookmarks.

- **Music.** You can opt to sync all your songs, music videos, and playlists here—or, if your collection is larger than the iPhone's capacity, just some of them.

- **Photos.** Here, you can get iPhone-friendly versions of your digital pictures copied over from a folder on your hard drive—or from a photo-management program like Photoshop Elements, Photoshop Album, or iPhoto.

- **Podcasts.** This screen lets you sync all—or just selected—podcasts. You can even opt to get only the unplayed ones from iTunes.

- **Videos.** You can choose both movies and TV shows from the iTunes Store for syncing here, along with other compatible video files in your library.

At the bottom of the screen, iTunes displays a colorful horizontal map that shows you the amount and types of files: Audio, Video, Photos, and Other (for your personal data). More importantly, it also shows you how much room you have left to wedge even more stuff onto your little black-and-chrome traveling companion.

The following pages detail how to sync each kind of iPhone-friendly material onto your phone: music, audio books, podcasts, videos, photos, contacts, calendars, bookmarks, and email account settings.

Syncing Music and Audio Books

The iTunes preferences give you two separate tabs for transferring your audio files to the iPhone: Music and Podcasts. The iPhone must be connected to the computer and showing in the iTunes window. Click the iPhone icon when you see it.

To copy over the music and audio books you want to take along on your phone, click the Music tab in the main part of the iTunes window. Next, turn on Sync Music. Now you need to decide *how much* music to put on your phone.

- If you have a big iPhone and a small music library, you can opt to sync "All songs and playlists" with one click.

- If you have a big music collection and want to take only *some* of it along for the iPhone ride, click "Selected playlists." In the window below, turn on the checkboxes for the playlists you want to transfer. If you don't have any playlists yet, flip back to Chapter 10 for instructions.

Audio books, like music videos, already live on their own self-titled playlists. Click the appropriate checkbox to include them in your sync.

Making It All Fit

Sooner or later, everybody has to confront the fact that the iPhone holds only 4 or 8 gigabytes of music and video. (Actually, only 3.3 or 7.3 gigs, because the operating system itself eats up 700 megabytes!) That's enough for 800 or 1,800 songs or so—assuming you don't put any video or photos on there.

Your multimedia stash is probably bigger than that. If you just turn on all "Sync All" checkboxes, then, you'll get an error message telling you that it won't all fit on the iPhone.

One way to solve the problem is to tiptoe through the Music, Podcasts, Photos, and Videos tabs, turning off checkboxes and trying to sync until the "too much" error message goes away.

Another helpful approach is to use the *smart playlist*, a music playlist that assembles itself based in criteria that you supply. For example:

❶ **In iTunes, choose File→New Smart Playlist.** The Smart Playlist dialog box appears.

❷ **Specify the category.** Use the pop-up menus to choose, for example, a musical genre, or songs you've played recently, or *haven't* played recently, or that you've rated highly.

❸ **Turn on the "Limit to" checkbox, and set up the constraints.** For example, you could limit the amount of music in this playlist to 2 giga-bytes, chosen at random. That way, every time you sync, you'll get a fresh random supply of songs on your iPhone, with enough room left for some videos.

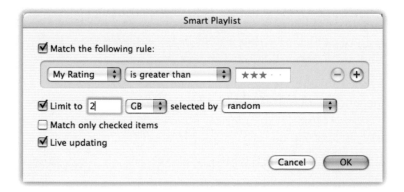

❹ **Click OK.** The new Smart Playlist appears in your Source list, where you can rename it.

Click it to look it over, if you like. Then, on the Music tab, choose this playlist for syncing to the iPhone.

Syncing Podcasts

You get a special Podasts tab in iTunes just for your podcast management on the iPhone. Once you click that Podcasts tab, you can choose to sync all shows, selected shows, all unplayed episodes—or just a certain number of episodes per sync. Individual checkboxes let you choose *which* podcast series get to come along for the ride.

Syncing Video

When it assumes the role of an iPod, one of the things the iPhone does best

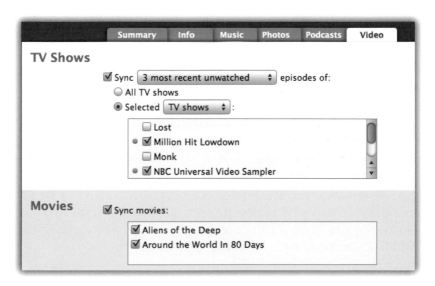

is play video on its gorgeous, glossy screen. TV shows and movies purchased from the iTunes Store look especially nice, since they're formatted with iPods in mind.

Syncing TV shows and movies works just like syncing music or podcasts. Connect the iPhone and click its icon in iTunes. Click the Videos tab in the main window, and then check the sync options and video files you want to transfer in the list below. Finally, click Apply to sync up.

Syncing Photos (Computer→iPhone)

Why corner people with your wallet to look at your kid's baby pictures, when you can whip out your iPhone and dazzle them with a finger-tapping slide-show? iTunes can sync the photos from your hard drive onto the iPhone, too. If you use a compatible photo-management program, you can even select individual albums of images that you've already assembled on your computer. Your photo-filling options for the iPhone include:

- **Photoshop Elements 3.0 or later** for Windows.

- **Photoshop Album 2.0 or later** for Windows.

- **iPhoto 4.0.3 or later** on the Mac.

- **Aperture**, Apple's high-end program for photography pros with muscular Macs.

- **Any folder of photos on your hard drive**, like My Pictures (in Windows), Pictures (on the Mac), or any folder you like.

The common JPEG files generated by just about every digital camera work just fine for iPhone photos. The GIF and PNG files used by Web pages work, too.

 Note You can sync photos from only one computer. If you later attempt to snag some snaps from a second machine, iTunes warns you that you must first erase all the images that came from the *original* computer.

When you're ready to sync your photos, connect the iPhone, click the iPhone icon in the iTunes source list, and then click the Photos tab in the main part of the window. Turn on "Sync photos," and then indicate where you'd like to sync them *from* (Photoshop Elements, iPhoto, or whatever).

If you want only some of the albums from your photo-shoebox software, turn on their checkboxes. Once you make your selections and click Apply in the lower-right corner of the iTunes window, the program bustles around "optimizing" copies of your photos to make them look great on the iPhone (for example, downsizing them from 10-megapixel overkill to something more appropriate for a 0.15-megapixel screen) and then ports them over.

After the sync is complete, you'll be able to wave your iPhone around, and people will *beg* to see your photos.

Syncing Photos (iPhone→Computer)

The previous discussion describes copying photos only in one direction: Computer→iPhone. But here's one of those rare instances when you can actually *create* data on the iPhone so that you can later transfer it to the computer: photos you take with the iPhone's own camera. You can rest easy, knowing that they can be copied back to your computer for safekeeping, with only one click.

Now, it's important to understand that *iTunes is not involved* in this process. It doesn't know anything about photos coming *from* the iPhone; its job is just to copy pictures *to* the iPhone.

So what's handling the iPhone→computer transfer? Your operating system. It sees the iPhone as though it's a digital camera, and suggests importing them just as it would from a camera's memory card.

Here's how it goes: put the iPhone into its cradle. What you'll see is probably something like this:

- **On the Macintosh,** iPhoto opens. This free photo-organizing/editing software comes on every Mac. Shortly after it notices that the iPhone is on the premises, it goes into Import mode.

Turn on "Delete photos after importing" if you'd like the iPhone's camera-phone memory cleared out after the transfer.

Either way, click Import on the Mac screen to begin the transfer.

- **In Windows.** When you attach a camera (or an iPhone), a dialog box pops up that asks how you want them handled. It lists any photo-management program you might have installed (Picasa, Photoshop Elements, Photoshop Album, and so on), as well as Windows' own camera-management software ("Scanner and Camera Wizard" in Windows XP; "using Windows" in Vista).

  Click the program you want to handle importing the iPhone pictures. You'll probably also want to turn on "Always use this program for this action," so the next time, it'll happen automatically without your having to fool around with a dialog box.

Shutting Up the Importing Process

Then again, some iPhone owners would rather *not* see some lumbering photo-management program firing itself up every time they connect the phone. You, too, might wish there were a way to *stop* iPhoto or Windows from bugging you every time you connect the iPhone.

That, too, is easy enough to change—if you know where to look.

- **Windows XP.** With the iPhone connected, choose Start→My Computer. Right-click the iPhone's icon. From the shortcut menu, choose Properties. Click the Events tab; click "Take no action." Click OK.

- **Windows Vista.** When the AutoPlay dialog box appears, click "Set AutoPlay defaults in Control Panel." (Or, if the AutoPlay dialog box is no longer on the screen, choose Start→Control Panel→AutoPlay.)

Windows Vista

Windows XP

Scroll all the way to the bottom, until you see the iPhone icon. From the pop-up menu, choose "Take no action." Click Save.

- **Macintosh.** Open Applications→Image Capture. Choose Image Capture→Preferences. Click CDs & DVDs. Where it says "When a camera is connected, open:", choose "No application." Click OK.

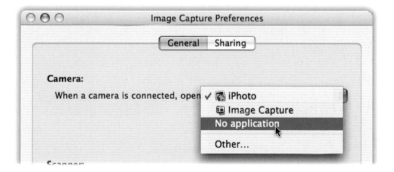

From now on, no photo-importing message will appear when you set the iPhone in the cradle. (You can always import its photos manually, of course.)

Syncing Contacts

If you've been adding to your address book for years in a program like Microsoft Outlook or Mac OS X's Address Book, you're just a sync away from porting all that accumulated data right over to your iPhone. Once there, info like phone numbers and email addresses show up as links, so you can reach out and tap someone.

Here's how to sync up your contacts with the iPhone. The steps are slightly different depending on which program you keep them in.

Outlook 2003 and 2007

With the iPhone plugged into the computer, click its icon in the iTunes source list, then click the Info tab in the main part of the window. Turn on *Sync contacts from:*, and, from the pop-up menu, choose *Outlook*. Finally, click Apply.

Note that some of the more obscure data fields Outlook lets you use, like "Radio" and "Telex," won't show up on the iPhone. All the major data points, however, like name, email address, and (most importantly) phone number, do.

If Outlook gives you grief and error messages, you might be missing the necessary plug-in. Visit *http://tinyurl.com/2lff4y* for Apple's tips on getting it to play nice with the iPhone.

Outlook Express

Microsoft's free email app for Windows stores your contacts in a file called the Windows Address Book. With the iPhone plugged into the computer, click its icon in the iTunes source list, and then click the Info tab in the main part of the window.

Turn on *Sync contacts from:*, choose *Windows Address Book* from the pop-up menu, and click Apply.

Windows Mail

Windows Mail, included with Windows Vista, is essentially a renamed version of Outlook Express. You set it up to sync with the iPhone's Contacts program just as described in the previous paragraphs—except in iTunes, choose *Windows Contacts*, rather than Windows Address Book, before clicking Apply.

Yahoo Address Book

The Yahoo Address Book is the address book component of a free Yahoo Mail account. It's therefore an *online* address book, which has certain advantages—like your ability to access it from any computer on the Internet.

Plug the iPhone into the computer, click its icon in the iTunes source list, and then click the Info tab in the main part of the window. Turn on *Sync contacts from:*, and choose *Yahoo Address Book* from the pop-up menu. (On the Mac, just turn on Yahoo Address Book; no menu is needed.)

Since Yahoo is an *online* address book, you need an Internet connection and your Yahoo ID and password to sync it with the iPhone. Click *Configure*, and then type your Yahoo ID and password. When finished, click OK. Now click Apply in the bottom corner of the iTunes window to get syncing.

Because it's online, syncing your Yahoo address book has a couple of other quirks. They're a little bit tweaky and geeky, but here they are for the record:

- Ordinarily, if you sync your iPhone with one contacts program and later try to sync with another one, iTunes asks if you want to **replace** the original list of contacts or **merge** the new ones with the ones already on the iPhone.

  But when you choose Yahoo's address book as the new source, you're offered only the Merge option.

- Usually, if you delete a name from your Mac or PC address book, it gets deleted from the iPhone the next time you sync. But if you delete a contact from the Yahoo Address Book that happens to contain a Yahoo Messenger ID in its fields, it **won't** disappear from the iPhone. To delete such a contact, you have to log onto your Yahoo account online and delete it from the Yahoo address book itself.

Mac OS X Address Book

Apple products generally love each other, and the built-in contact keeper that comes with Mac OS X is a breeze to sync up with your iPhone. With the iPhone plugged into the computer, click its icon in the iTunes source list, and then click the Info tab in the main part of the window. Turn on Turn on *Sync contacts from:*, and pick *Address Book* from the pop-up menu.

If you've gathered sets of people together as **groups** in your address book, you can also transfer them to the iPhone in their groups by turning on *selected groups* and checking off the ones you want. When finished, click Apply to sync things up.

Entourage 2004

Entourage, Microsoft's email program for the Mac, also plays nice with the iPhone, as long as you introduce it properly first.

In Entourage, choose Entourage→Preferences. Under General Preferences, choose Sync Services. Turn on *Synchronize services with Address Book and .Mac*.

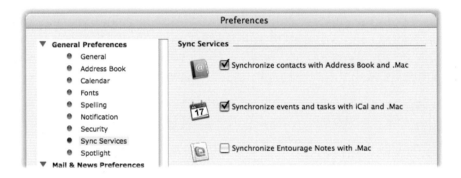

Click OK, and then plug the iPhone into the computer. Click its icon in the iTunes source list, and then click the Info tab in the main part of the window. Turn on *Sync contacts from:*, and, from the pop-up menu, choose *Address Book*. Finally, click Apply to sync.

Other Programs

Even if you still keep your contacts in a Jurassic-era program like Palm Desktop 4.1, you may still be able to get them into the iPhone/iTunes sync dance. If you can export your contacts as vCards (a contacts-exchange format with the extension .vcf), you can import them into the Windows Address Book or the Mac's Address Book.

In Palm Desktop 4.1 for the Mac, for instance, choose File→Export→ Addresses, select vCard for the export format, and then click OK. Export the file to your desktop, open the Mac Address Book, and then **import** the same file.

It's trickier on the PC version of Palm Desktop 4.1, since you can only export one contact at a time. But a handy little freeware program called Palm2iPod can do it all for you. It's available from the "Missing CD-ROM" page at *www.missingmanuals.com*.

Now you can sync to your heart's delight.

Syncing Bookmarks

Bookmarks—those helpful little point-and-click shortcuts that have saved us all countless hours of mistyping Web site addresses—are a reflection of your personality, because they generally tend to be sites that are important to *you*. Fortunately, they can make the trip to your iPhone, too. In fact, any bookmarks you create on the iPhone can eventually be copied back to your computer, too; it's a two-way street.

iTunes can transfer your bookmarks from Internet Explorer or Safari (Windows), or from the Safari browser on a Mac. Just plug in the iPhone, click its icon in iTunes, and click the Info tab. Scroll down past Contacts and Calendars and Mail Accounts until you get to the section called Web Browser. Then:

- **In Windows,** turn on *Sync bookmarks from:*, and then choose either *Safari* or *Internet Explorer* from the pop-up menu. Click Apply to sync.

- **On the Mac,** turn on *Sync Safari bookmarks* and click Apply.

Special Instructions for Firefox Fans

If Mozilla's Firefox browser is your preferred window to the Web, you can still get those foxy favorites moved over to the iPhone. But you'll have to do it the long way—by importing bookmarks from Firefox into Safari. And while this setup will get your bookmarks onto the iPhone, it won't establish a living, *two-way* sync; new bookmarks you add on the iPhone won't get synced back to Firefox.

- **Windows.** Download a free copy of Safari *www.apple.com/safari*, start it up, and let it import your Firefox bookmarks during the setup process.

Once it does, press Ctrl+Alt+B to show all your bookmarks, weed out the ones you don't want, and then set the iPhone to sync with Safari.

- **Macintosh.** You already have a copy of Safari. If you have your whole bookmarked life in Firefox, grit your teeth and open that dusty Safari anyway, then choose the File→Import Bookmarks. Navigate to your Firefox bookmarks file, which is usually in your Home folder→Library→Application Support→Firefox→Profiles→*weird scrambled-named folder like e9v01wmx.default* folder. Inside, double-click the file called bookmarks. html.

    You've just imported your Firefox bookmarks. Now, in Safari, press ⌘-Option-B to show all your bookmarks on screen. Delete the ones you don't want on the iPhone, and then set the iPhone to sync with Safari.

Actually, *most* other browsers can export their bookmarks. You can use that option to export your bookmarks file to your desktop, and then use Safari's File→Import Bookmarks menu to pull it from there.

Syncing Your Calendar

With its snazzy-looking calendar program tidily synced with your computer, the iPhone can keep you on schedule—and even remind you when you have to call a few people.

Out of the box, the iPhone's calendar works with Outlook 2003 and 2007 for Windows, and iCal and Entourage 2004 on the Mac.

The iPhone's calendar program isn't especially full-featured, however. For example, it doesn't have to-do lists, which *should* be on the to-do lists of the folks at Apple's iPhone Software Headquarters. The iPhone can't handle multiple categories, either—different colors so you can tell what part of your life is on what schedule. Otherwise, it's very pretty and it does generally keep you on track.

Here again, setting up the sync depends on the calendar program you're now using on your computer.

 Note If you have Windows Vista, you have a built-in calendar program—Windows Calendar—but no way to sync it with the iPhone. The reason, according to Apple, is that Microsoft has not made public the format of its calendar program.

Outlook 2003/2007 Calendar (Windows)

Plug your iPhone into the PC and wait for it to pop up in iTunes. Click its icon in the iTunes source list. Next, click the Info tab in the main part of the iTunes window. In the Calendars area, turn on "Sync calendars from Outlook."

You can also choose how many days' worth of old events you want to have on your pocket calendar, since you probably rarely need to reference, say, your calendar from 2002. Turn on "Do not sync events older than [blank] days," and then specify the number of days' worth of old appointments you want to have on hand.

Events that you tap into the iPhone get carried back to Outlook when you reconnect to the computer and sync up.

iCal (Macintosh)

Mac OS X comes with a nimble little datebook called iCal, which syncs right up with the iPhone. To use it, plug your iPhone into the Mac and wait for it to pop up in iTunes. Click its icon in the iTunes source list. Click the Info tab in the main part of the iTunes window. In the Calendars area, turn on "Sync iCal calendars."

If you have several different calendars (color-coded categories) in iCal—Work, Home, Book Club and so on—you can turn on "Selected calendars" and choose the ones you want to copy to the iPhone. Be warned, though: The color coding in iCal all turns into basic gray on the iPhone, so you can't tell what appointment is from which calendar.

Tip The calendar on the iPhone doesn't offer that "calendars" (categories) feature. All appointments that you create on the iPhone belong, in essence, to the same calendar.

But which one would you like that *one* to be? That is, when you sync the iPhone with your Mac, which category should those new events belong to?

Make your decision by choosing the category's name from the "Put new events created on this iPhone" pop-up menu.

Near the bottom of the calendar-sync preferences, there's a place to indicate how far back you want to sync old events.

Once you get all your calendar preferences set up the way you like, click Apply in the bottom of the iTunes window to get your schedule in sync.

Entourage (Mac)

Entourage can sync its calendar events with the iPhone, too. Start by opening Entourage, and then choose Entourage→Preferences. Under General Preferences, choose Sync Services and turn on "Synchronize events and tasks with iCal and .Mac" (see page 220). Click OK, and then plug the iPhone into the computer.

Click the iPhone icon in the iTunes source list, and then click the Info tab in the main part of the window. Turn on "Sync iCal calendars" and click the Apply button to sync.

 Tip If you're a Mac fan, and you live your life according to the Google Calendar, you can live it up on the iPhone courtesy of a little program called Spanning Sync (*www.spanningsync.com*). For $25 a year (or a one-time $65), the software syncs up events created in Google's online datebook program with iCal on the Mac. And from there, getting them on the iPhone is just a hop, skip, and a click away.

Syncing Email Settings

Teaching a new computer of *any* sort to get and send your email can be stressful; the job entails plugging all sorts of user-hostile information bits called things like SMTP Server Address and Uses SSL. Presumably, though, you've got your email working on your Mac or PC—wouldn't it be great if you didn't have to duplicate all that work on your iPhone?

That's exactly what iTunes can do for you. It can transfer the *account setup information* to the iPhone, so that it's ready to start dialing for messages immediately.

It can do that *if*, that is, your current email program is Mail or Entourage (on the Mac) or Outlook or Outlook Express (in Windows).

Start by plugging the iPhone into the computer. In iTunes, click the iPhone's icon and then click the Info tab in the main part of the window. Scroll on down to Mail Accounts. The next step varies by operating system:

- **Windows.** Turn on "Sync selected mail accounts from:" and, from the shortcut menu, choose Outlook or Outlook Express.

- **Macintosh.** Turn on "Sync selected Mail accounts."

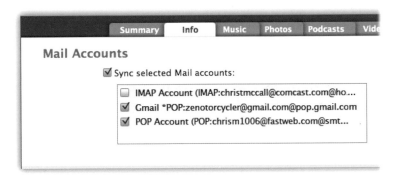

Finally, if your email program collects messages from multiple accounts, turn on the checkboxes of the accounts you want to see on your iPhone. Click Apply to start syncing.

 Note This business of transferring email settings doesn't always go smoothly, at least in iPhone 1.0. Mac fans have learned, for example, that Mail transfers your settings more successfully than Entourage. And Windows Vista fans have discovered that even though Windows Mail is just a renamed, updated version of Outlook Express, iTunes isn't especially friendly with it.

Syncing With Multiple Computers

In general, Apple likes to keep things simple. Everything it ever says about the iPhone suggests that you can sync only *one* iPhone with *one* computer.

That's only half true, however.

Yes, you can sync only *one* iPhone at a time to a Mac or PC. But you can actually sync the same iPhone with *multiple* Macs or PCs.

And why would you want to do that? So that you can fill it up with material from different places: music and video from a Mac at home; contacts and calendar from your Windows PC at work; and maybe even the photos from your laptop.

iTunes derives these goodies from different sources to begin with—pictures from your photo program, addresses and appointments from your contacts and calendar programs, music and video from iTunes. So all you have to do is set up the tabs of each computer's copy of iTunes to sync *only* one kind of material.

On the Mac, for example, you'd turn off the Sync checkboxes on all tabs except Music, Podcasts, and Video. Sync away.

Then take the iPhone to the office; on your PC, turn off the Sync checkboxes on all tabs except Info. Sync away once more.

Then on the laptop, turn off Sync on all tabs except Photos.

And off you go. Each time you connect the iPhone to one of the computers, it syncs that data set according to the preferences set in that copy of iTunes.

 Tip How's this for an undocumented secret? You can use the iPhone to *combine* several different address books—Outlook on a PC and Address Book on a Mac, for example. *All* your contacts wind up on *all* machines—iPhone, Mac, and PC.

Suppose you've synced the iPhone with Computer #1. When you plug it into Computer #2, click the iPhone icon and then the Info tab. Select the additional program you want to sync from—Outlook, Yahoo, whatever. Click Apply.

When iTunes asks if you want to Merge Info or Replace Info, click Merge Info. Now all of the iPhone's existing addresses remain in your current address book, but it also copies the contacts from the second computer to the iPhone.

Conflicts

If you use only one machine at a time, you'll never have **conflicts**. You'll never change your dentist appointment to 3:00 p.m. on the iPhone, but change it to 4:00 p.m. on your computer, between syncs. Or you'd never edit a phone number in Contacts simultaneously in two different ways on the two different machines. One machine would always be the "hot potato."

In the real world, though, conflicts occasionally happen. Fortunately, iTunes is pretty smart about handling them. If it discovers that, since the last sync, you've edited a single phone number or appointment in two different ways (one each on the iPhone and your computer), it lets you know with a message box.

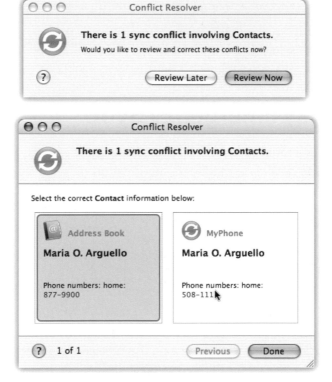

Note If you edit two *different* phone numbers on a single person's card—like a cellphone number on the PC, and a fax number on the iPhone—that doesn't count as a conflict. Both machines will inherit both phone numbers.

iTunes considers it a conflict, and asks you to settle it, only when two changes were made to the *same* phone number.

You're offered two buttons:

- **Review Later.** This button actually means, "the computer's version wins." There's actually no way to review the conflict later.

- **Review Now.** You're shown the two changes, side-by-side, in a window. Click the one you think seems more authoritative; that's the one that will wind up prevailing on both machines. Then click Done.

Of course, the computer has to sync one more time to apply the change you've indicated. On the Mac, you're offered buttons that say Sync Now or Sync Later; in Windows, the buttons say Sync Now or Cancel (meaning "not now"). In both cases, you should click Sync Now to avoid confusion.

One-Way Emergency Sync

In general, the iPhone's ability to handle bidirectional syncs is a blessing. It means that whenever you modify the information on one of your beloved machines, you won't have to duplicate that effort on the other one. It also makes possible that multi-computer address-book merging trick described in the previous pages.

It can also get hairy. Depending on what merging, fussing, and button-clicking you do, it's possible to make a mess of your iPhone's address book or calendar. You could fill it with duplicate entries, or the wrong entries, or entries from a computer that you didn't intend to merge in there.

Fortunately, as a last resort, iTunes offers a *forced one-way sync* option, which makes your computer's version of things the official one. Everything on the iPhone will get replaced by the computer's version, just this once. At least you'll know exactly where all that information came from.

To do an emergency one-way sync, set the iPhone into its cradle. Click its icon in iTunes. On the Info tab, scroll all the way to the bottom, until you see the Advanced area. There it is: "Replace the information on this iPhone," complete with checkboxes for the four things that iTunes can completely replace on the phone: Contacts, Calendars, Mail Accounts, or Bookmarks. Click the Apply button to start fresh.

12

Add-Ons: Accessories and Web Apps

When Steve Jobs announced, shortly before the iPhone went on sale, that programmers wouldn't be able to write new programs for it, there was much muttering. "It's a *computer*, for the love of Mike," went the refrain. "It runs Mac OS X! Let us write new programs!"

Apple says it's only trying to preserve the stability of the phone and of the AT&T network. But the company decided to allow programmers one little bit of freedom: They could write special *Web-based* programs tailored for the iPhone.

These programs will never show up as icons on your Home screen, and you can get to them only when you're online, but still, the creativity and usefulness out there is amazing. Hundreds of Web-based programs—most of them free—let you pull down movie listings, the nearest place to get cheap gas, the latest headlines, and so on. You can even connect to rudimentary instant-messenger programs to enhance your iPhone experience.

Those are just the *software* add-ons. There's also a world of accessories for the outside of the iPhone: cases, headsets, chargers, and other goodies. This chapter gives you a sampling of both kinds of add-ons and suggests where you can go to find out what's new in iPhone Web apps and gear.

Web Applications

Thanks to the efforts of creative programmers who got started even before the phone hit the stores, the iPhone has the potential to run thousands of programs in its wee Web browser.

Some iPhone Web applications look like Mac OS X or Yahoo desktop widgets that do one thing really well—like showing you a Doppler radar map for your local weather. Some are mini-pages that tap directly into popular social networking sites like Flickr and Twitter. Some even let you tap into Web-based word processing sites if you need to create a document *right this very instant*.

You get to any Web app the same way: Punch up Safari on the iPhone and tap in the Web address for the application's site. If you like it, find it useful, and want to go back again, just bookmark it.

You can find iPhone apps in just about every category. Some examples:

Word Processors

Need to dash off a document on the run? Word processing and office programs that work right off the Web can do in a pinch—no hard drive required. They go way beyond the iPhone's simple Notes program.

- **iZoho iPhone Office.** The folks behind Zoho Writer, a popular Web-based collaboration site, have an iPhone-ready version of their online word processing, spreadsheet, and presentation programs. You need to sign up for a free account, but after that you can create documents and store them on the site for later retrieval. *(http://mini.zoho.com)*

- **gOffice for iPhone.** Believe it or not, this site lets you create Microsoft Word documents right on your phone. gOffice even stocks several time-saving text templates. Your documents are plastered with a gOffice logo and iPhone image—but hey, it's free. You can email the documents right from your iPhone, or for $3, the gOffice office will print out your missive (up to five pages) and send it by good old-fashioned snail mail to an address you provide. *(http://goffice.com)*

 Note The most famous online office suite, Google Docs (word processor) and Google Spreadsheets, weren't iPhone-compatible on iPhone Day One. But Google says that it intends to remedy that situation. Once it does, these Google apps will offer yet another tool for on-the-go writing and number crunching.

News Readers

Keep up with the world from all your favorite sources, from mainstream media sites like the BBC and *New York Times* to your favorite blog about fire-breathing. Piped in by *RSS feeds* (page 133), these short nuggets of news give you the headlines and a quick overview, along with links to the full story.

- **iActu.** A gorgeous little virtual newsstand appears on your iPhone screen when you visit iActu, complete with tiny images of popular newspapers.

Tap a paper (*USA Today*, *Wall Street Journal*, and *Los Angeles Times* are among the choices) to read the headlines and summaries from each one's top stories. *(www.widgetinfo.net/iphone/)*

- **Google Reader.** The big G's popular news roundup service comes to the iPhone. Just like its big-boy version for regular Web browsers, Google's RSS reader scours the Web for news from all corners. You can get feeds from tech blogs like Lifehacker, Engadget, and Slashdot, as well as sports news from ESPN.com, financial news from MarketWatch.com, and snarky humor from *The Onion*.

   To get started, visit Google.com and sign up for a free Google account. (If you've used Gmail or another Google service, you already have one.) After you set up your reader options, you can use the same name and password to log in and read your feeds on your phone. *(www.google.com/reader)*

Mobile Helpers for Major Sites

Among the new iPhone apps are some especially efficient ways to hop a quick ride to some of your favorite Web sites.

- **TeleMoose.** Forget about waiting around for Amazon's site to load on the iPhone, especially if you're already on the ledge with EDGE. Let TeleMoose whisk you to its streamlined edition of the Web superstore.

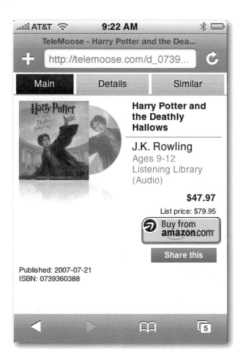

Tap a product category to shop Amazon's virtual aisles. *(www.telemoose. com)*

- **iPhlickr.** As the site itself puts it, "iPhone + Flickr = iPhlickr." This app gives you a phone-sized window into the vast Flickr.com photo-sharing site. With simple search options right on the main page, iPhlickr lets you view your own photos, find pictures by specific Flickr members (by tag), and check out recently added snaps. *(www.chandlerkent.com/iphlickr)*

- **Ta-da Lists.** The iPhone may be missing a to-do list function in its own toolbox, but don't let that stop you. You can create your own list of must-dos on the Ta-da Lists site when you sign up for a free account. *(tadalist. com/iphone)*

iPhone Application Launchers

With all the new programs popping up every week, all-in-one sites to *manage* or *launch* your iPhone applications are a great way to corral a bunch of them at once. Once you set up an account or customize an application manager site, you can bookmark it and easily bop around to your favorite programs from its main screen. Notable iPhone application launchers include:

- **MockDock.** You sign up with just an email address. Then, from a big collection of different programs, start filling your new home screen by tapping the icons you want to add. Among the offerings: Games (sudoku, chess), social networking sites (Twitter, Facebook), and plenty of great utility programs like a mileage tracker, the 101 Cookbooks recipe database, and news readers. *(mockdock.com)*

- **iPhoneAppsManager.** This site had 66 apps in place only a week after the iPhone arrived. It skips the little widget-like icons in favor of an elegant text-based interface that groups applications into categories like Games & Fun, News, Search Tools, Utilities, and so on. On the main screen, you can tap apps to add to a Favorites list. *(iphoneappsmanager.com)*

- **AppMarks.** A tip calculator, a cheap-gas finder, and Yahoo Mobile are among the useful apps here. And if you don't find enough to suit you, AppMarks lets you add any Web site to your personalized page. Just create a free account and sign on to see your chosen apps. *(appmarks.com)*

- **Mojits.** Big bright icons point the way to several popular iPhone apps, including a detailed AccuWeather map; sites for getting local movie times; and quick trips to Twitter, Digg, and Flickr. *(www.mojits.com/home)*

- **Widgetop.** Billing itself as "Your Web Desktop," Widgetop brings together a collection of fun and helpful iPrograms, including shortcuts to Wikipedia, Mac-like sticky notes, and even an app whose sole function is to offer quotes from *The Big Lebowski*. *(m.widgetop.com)*

iPhone Accessories

When it comes to hardware attachments and accessories, many people assume that anything that works for an iPod will work on the iPhone. After all, the iPhone is just another iPod, right?

Not!

For example:

- The iPhone's dimensions are different from the iPods that came before it, so regular iPod cases don't fit.

- The iPhone's headphone jack is recessed, so regular headphone stereo miniplugs don't fully connect.

- The iPhone is also a phone, with components inside that can cause static, buzz, and interference when used with external speakers (which have their own electronic innards).

- The iPhone can play video like an iPod, but unlike an iPod, it doesn't have any kind of video output feature. So home-entertainment docks designed to connect the player with a television don't work.

To help shoppers get products that are compatible with the iPhone, Apple has its own "Works with iPhone" logo program. As the company puts it, products bearing the logo are "electronic accessories designed to connect specifically to iPhone and certified by the developer to meet Apple performance standards."

Getting stuff with the "Works with iPhone" logo should save you the grief that comes with "Buying the Wrong Thing." And if you're looking for iPhone-friendly accessories, several companies already have plenty of products to sell you. Some good places to look include:

- **Apple's iPhone Accessories page.** Here you can find all those official white plastic cables, docks, and power adapters, plus Bluetooth headsets and more. *(www.apple.com/iphone/accessories)*

- **Digital Lifestyle Outfitters.** DLO has been turning out handsome iPod cases practically since the little white MP3 player took the first spin of its scroll wheel, and they had cases and other accessories in stock before the iPhone hit the street. *(www.dlo.com)*

- **XtremeMac.** Another iPod stuffmaker. XtremeMac makes fashionable car chargers and other powerful products that work with the iPhone. *(www. xtrememac.com)*

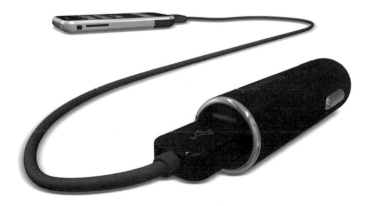

- **Griffin Technology.** Offers cables and cases for the iPhone along with many other audio accessories. *(www.griffintechnology.com)*

- **Belkin.** From acrylic cases to sporty armbands, Belkin markets several iPhone items, including an adapter for that hard-to-reach headphone port. *(www.belkin.com)*

- **EverythingiPhone.** If it works with an iPhone, you can probably find it here by clicking the Store tab. This virtual iPhone mall has cleaning cloths, screen protectors, Bluetooth headsets, cases, and more. And it's not just a shopping center—user forums, reviews, and news make the site live up to its all-encompassing name. *(www.everythingiphone.com)*

iPod Accessories

Picking products with the "Works with iPhone" logo ensures happy shopping, but your existing iPod gear *might* play nice with iPhone. If you're game, keep the following advice in mind.

External Speakers

Most speaker sets that connect through the 30-pin port on the bottom of modern iPods also fit iPhone. You may need one of Apple's Universal Dock adapters—a white plastic booster seat that makes most iPod models sit securely in speaker docks—for a good fit. (And frankly, external woofers and tweeters sound infinitely better than the iPhone's tiny, tinny speaker when you really want to rock out.)

One major thing to remember, though: electronic interference. If you forget, the iPhone will remind you. If it senses you're seating it in a non-"Works with iPhone" speaker system, you'll see a message suggesting that you put it in Airplane mode. Doing so takes care of the interference, but it also prevents you for making or getting phone calls. You can blow by the warning and keep Airplane mode off, but you may get some unwanted static blasts with your music.

FM Transmitters

Those little gadgets that broadcast your iPod's music to an empty frequency on your dashboard radio are a godsend for iPodders who don't want to listen to the same 40 songs over and over on commercial radio. Unfortunately, these transmitters are not so hot for the iPhone. Again, electronic interference is an issue, unless you put the phone into Airplane mode. Transmitters that connect through the headphone jack, meanwhile, probably won't fit.

Earphones

If you've ditched your telltale white iPod earphones for a higher fidelity head-set, you probably won't be able to connect it to the iPhone's sunken head-phone jack. Fortunately, Belkin and other manufacturers have come up with inexpensive jack adapters that bridge the gap between port and plug.

 Note Speaking of audio, see page 68 for a discussion of Bluetooth wireless headsets for the iPhone.

Protecting Your iPhone

With its glass-and-chrome good looks, keeping the iPhone from getting scuffed, scratched, or dented is a priority for many people who've just dropped $500 or $600 on the thing. Two accessories in particular can bring an extra layer of protection (and peace of mind): cases and screen protectors.

Cases

Tucking your iPhone inside a leather or rubber covering can make it easier to handle as well as helping it hold up inside your pocket or purse. When you shop for a case, keep in mind the ways you use your iPhone. Into sports and activity? Perhaps a brightly colored rubberized covering that lets you dial without taking it out of the case would work best. Using it as you stroll around the office all day? Consider a smart leather holster-style case with a belt clip.

Screen Protectors

People who've used stylus-based Palms, Pocket PCs, or smartphones are big fans of screen protectors—thin sheets of sticky plastic that lie smoothly over the glass to provide a protective barrier. Many iPhone accessory shops (page 237) sell screen protectors customized to fit perfectly over the phone's touch-sensitive side.

13 Settings

Y our iPhone is a full-blown computer—well, at least a half-blown one. And like any good computer, it's customizable. The Settings application, right there on your Home screen, is like the Control Panel in Windows, or System Preferences on the Mac. It's a tweaking center that affects every aspect of the iPhone: the screen, ringtones, email, Web connection, and so on.

You scroll the Settings list as you would any iPhone list: by dragging your finger up or down the screen.

Most of the items on the Settings page are doorways to other screens, where you make the actual changes. When you're finished inspecting or changing the preference settings, you return to the main Settings screen by tapping the Settings button in the upper-left corner.

In this book, you can read about the iPhone's preference settings in the appropriate spots—wherever they're relevant. But just so you'll have it all in one place, here's an item-by-item walkthrough of the Settings application .

Airplane Mode

As you're probably aware, you're not allowed to use cellphones on airplanes. According to legend (if not science), a cellphone's radio can interfere with a plane's navigation equipment.

But the iPhone does a lot more than make calls. Are you supposed to deprive yourself of all the music, videos, movies, and email that you could be answering in flight, just because cellphones are forbidden?

Nope. Just turn on Airplane mode by tapping the Off button at the top of the Settings list (so that the orange On button appears). Now it's safe (and permitted) to use the iPhone in flight—at least after takeoff, when you hear the announcement about "approved electronics"—because the cellular and Wi-Fi features of the iPhone are turned off completely. You can't make calls or get online, but you can do anything else in the iPhone's bag of non-wireless tricks.

Wi-Fi

Wi-Fi—wireless Internet networking—is one of the iPhone's best features. This item in Settings opens the Wi-Fi Networks screen, where you'll find three useful controls:

- **Wi-Fi On/Off.** If you don't plan to use Wi-Fi, turning it off gets you a lot more life out of each battery charge. Tap anywhere on this On/Off slider to change its status.

 Turning Airplane mode on automatically turns off the Wi-Fi antenna.

- **Choose a Network.** Here, you'll find a list of all nearby Wi-Fi networks that the iPhone can "see," complete with signal-strength indicator and a padlock icon if a password is required. An Other item lets you access Wi-Fi networks that are invisible and secret unless you know their names. See Chapter 6 for details on using Wi-Fi with the iPhone.

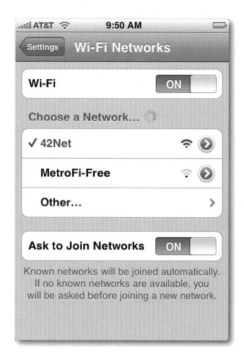

- **Ask to Join Networks.** If this option is On, then whenever you attempt to get online (to check email or the Web, for example), the iPhone sniffs around to find a Wi-Fi network. If it finds one you haven't used before, the iPhone invites you, with a small dialog box, to hop onto it.

  So why would you ever want to turn this feature off? To avoid getting bombarded with invitations to join Wi-Fi networks, which can happen in heavily populated areas, and to save battery power.

Carrier

If you see this panel at all, then you're doubly lucky. First, you're enjoying a trip overseas; second, you have a choice of cellphone carriers who have roaming agreements with AT&T. Tap your favorite, and prepare to pay some serious roaming fees.

Usage

In the months before the iPhone was released, Apple watchers whipped themselves into a frenzy of speculation about the iPhone's battery life. Wi-Fi, videos, Internet, cellphone calls—that's a lot of drain on a slim little internal battery. How would it do?

You probably already know the official Apple battery-life statistics: 8 hours of talking, or 6 hours of Internet, or 24 hours of music playing, and so on. But you don't have to trust Apple's figures, thanks to the handy built-in battery-life calculator shown here.

- **Time since last full charge.** The *Usage* readout shows, in hours and minutes, how much time you've spent using all iPhone functions (although it's not broken down by activity, alas). *Standby* is how much time the iPhone has spent in sleep mode, awaiting calls.

 The iPhone resets the Usage and Standby counters to zero each time you fully charge the battery.

- **Call Time.** These two statistics tell you how much time you've spent talking on the iPhone, broken down by Current Period (that is, during this AT&T billing month) and in the iPhone's entire existence. That's right, folks: For what's probably the first time in history, a cellphone actually keeps track of your minutes, to help you avoid exceeding the number you've signed up for (and therefore racking up 45-cent overage minutes).

- **EDGE Network Data.** These tallies indicate how much you've used the Internet, expressed as megabytes of data you've sent and received, including email messages and Web-page material. Unlike some cell-phone plans, which bill you by the megabyte (a virtually impossible-to-estimate statistic), you're getting unlimited Internet use for a flat fee. So make no attempt to throttle back on your Internet use; the Network Data stats are provided purely for your own amazement.

 Tip Tap Reset Statistics at the very bottom of the screen to set all Usage numbers back to zero.

Sounds

Here's a more traditional cellphone settings screen: the place where you choose a ringtone sound for incoming calls.

- **Silent Vibrate, Ring Vibrate.** Like any self-respecting cellphone, the iPhone has a Vibrate mode—a little shudder in your pocket that might get your attention when you can't hear the ringing. As you can see on this screen, there are two On/Off controls for the vibrator: one for when the phone is in Silent mode (page 12), and one for when the ringer's on.

- **Ring Volume.** The slider here controls the volume of the phone's ringing. Of course, it's usually faster to adjust the ring volume by pressing the up/down buttons on the left edge of the phone whenever you're not on a call.

- **Ringtone.** Tap this row to view the iPhone's list of 25 ringtones. (No, you can't use your own music as ringtones, and you can't download new ones.) Tap a ring sound to hear it. After you've tapped one that you like, confirm your choice by tapping the Sounds button at the top of the screen. You return to the Sounds screen.

Note Of course, you can choose a different ringtone for each person in your phone book (page 43).

- **New Voicemail, New Text Message, New Mail, Sent Mail…** These On/Off switches let you silence the little sounds that the iPhone plays to celebrate various events: the arrival of new voicemail, text messages, or mail; the successful sending of an outgoing email message; calendar events coming due; locking the iPhone by tapping the Sleep/Wake switch on the top of the phone; and typing on the virtual keyboard.

Brightness

Ordinarily, the iPhone controls its own screen brightness. An ambient-light sensor hidden behind the smoked glass at the top of the iPhone's face samples the room brightness each time you wake the phone, and adjusts the brightness automatically: brighter in bright rooms, dimmer in darker ones.

When you prefer more manual control, here's what you can do:

- **Brightness slider.** Drag the handle on this slider, or just tap on the slider, to control the screen brightness manually, keeping in mind that more brightness means shorter battery life.

  If Auto-Brightness is turned on, then the changes you make here are relative to the iPhone's self-chosen brightness. In other words, if you goose the brightness by 20 percent, the screen will always be 20 percent brighter than the iPhone would have chosen for itself.

- **Auto-Brightness On/Off.** Tap anywhere on this switch to disable the ambient-light sensor completely. Now the brightness of the screen is under complete manual control.

Wallpaper

Wallpaper just means the photo that appears on the Unlock screen, when you wake the iPhone up. You're not stuck with the Earth-from-Space photo forever (although it is a very nice piece of wallpaper).

To choose a different photo, tap the Wallpaper row. On the Wallpaper screen, you'll see at least three sub-items:

- **Wallpaper.** Tap this item to view the thumbnails of a set of luscious photos provided by Apple, including nature shots, flower closeups, the Mona Lisa, and Earth from Space.

- **Camera Roll.** Tap to see the thumbnails of any photos you've taken with the iPhone's built-in camera.

- **Albums.** The other occupants of this screen are listings of any photo albums you've synced onto your iPhone from your Mac or PC, as described on page 214. Tap an album name to view the thumbnails of its contents.

When you're viewing a page full of thumbnails, tap one to see a full-screen preview. At that point, tap Cancel to return to the thumbnails, or Set as Wallpaper to make that photo your new Unlock-screen masterpiece.

General

The General page offers a motley assortment of miscellaneous settings, governing the behavior of the virtual keyboard, the Bluetooth transmitter, the iPhone's little-known password-protection feature, and more.

- **About.** Tapping this item opens a page for the statistics nut. Here you can find out how many songs, videos, and photos your iPhone holds; how much storage your iPhone has, and how much of it you've used; and super-techie details like the iPhone's software and firmware versions, serial number, model, Wi-Fi and Bluetooth addresses, and so on. And when you're really bored, you can even tap Legal to open up some light reading, in the form of a 50-screen-tall list of copyright notices and disclaimers.

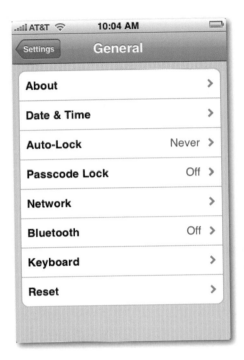

- **Date & Time.** At the top of this screen, you'll see an option to turn on "24-hour time," also known as military time, in which you see "1700" instead of "5:00 p.m." (You'll see this change everywhere times appear, including at the top edge of the screen.)

  "Set Automatically" refers to the iPhone's built-in clock. If this item is turned on, then the iPhone finds out what time it is from an atomic clock out on the Internet. If not, then you have to set the clock yourself. (Turning this option off makes two more rows of controls appear automatically: one for your time zone and a "number spinner" so you can set the clock.)

  As for the Calendar item, here's a mind-teaser for you world travelers. If an important event is scheduled for 6:30 p.m. New York time, and you're in California, how should that event appear on your calendar? Should it appear as 3:30 p.m. (that is, your local time)? Or should it remain stuck at 6:30 (East Coast time)?

It's not an idle question, because it also affects the iPhone's reminders and alarms.

Out of the box, Time Zone Support is turned on. That is, the iPhone automatically translates all your appointments into the local time. If you scheduled a reminder to record some TV movie at 8:00 p.m. New York time, and you're in California, the reminder will pop up at 5:00 p.m. local time.

 Note This presumes, of course, that the iPhone knows where you are. Even though the iPhone always knows what the local time is when you travel across time zones, it can't actually determine which time zone you're in. You have to tell it each time you change time zones—by tapping Time Zone here on this screen.

If you turn Time Zone Support off, then everything stays on the calendar just the way you entered it.

- **Auto-Lock.** As you may have noticed, the iPhone locks itself every time you put it to sleep (by tapping the top-edge Sleep/Wake button). It also locks after a few minutes of inactivity on your part. In locked mode, the iPhone ignores screen taps and button presses.

All cellphones (and iPods) offer locked mode. On this machine, however, locking is especially important because the screen is so big. Reaching into your pocket for a toothpick or ticket stub could theoretically fire up some iPhone program or even dial a call from the confines of your pocket.

On the Auto-Lock screen, you can change the interval of inactivity before the auto-lock occurs (1 minute, 2 minutes, and so on), or you can tap Never. In that case, the iPhone locks only when you send it to sleep—not automatically after an inactive period.

- **Passcode Lock.** This feature works exactly as it does on iPods. It lets you make up a four-digit password that you have to enter whenever you wake up the iPhone. If you don't know the password, you can't use the iPhone. It's designed to keep your stuff private from other people in the house or the office, or to protect your information in case you lose the iPhone.

To set up the password, type a four-digit number on the keypad. You're asked to do it again to make sure you didn't make a typo.

Once you confirm your password choice, you arrive at the Passcode Lock screen. Here, you can turn off the password requirement, change the number, and specify how quickly the password is requested before locking somebody out: immediately after the iPhone wakes, or a minute later. (That option was provided as a convenience to you, so you can quickly check your calendar or missed messages without having to enter the passcode—while still protecting your data from evildoers who steal your iPhone.)

Show SMS Preview is one final option here. If it's on, then you'll still be able to read any text messages that come in, even while the phone is protected by the passcode; they'll show up on the opening screen.

Note Don't kid around with this passcode. It's a much more serious deal than the iPod passcode. If you forget the iPhone code, you'll have to restore your iPhone (page 271), which wipes out everything on it. You've still got most of the data on your computer, of course (music, video, contacts, calendar), but you may lose text messages, mail, and so on.

- **Network.** Tap Network to open a screen containing two items.

  One is *VPN*, which stands for virtual private networking. In the corporate world, telecommuters often use VPN systems to "dial in" to their work computers from home. That, of course, involves getting through the company's firewall and other security measures. A VPN is a secure, encrypted tunnel that carries the data from one computer, across the Internet, and into the company's computers. Page 158 has the details for setting this up.

  The second item on the Network page is *Wi-Fi*, which is an exact duplicate of the Wi-Fi controls described on page 243.

- **Bluetooth.** There's nothing on this screen at first except an On/Off switch for the iPhone's Bluetooth transmitter, which is required to communicate with a Bluetooth earpiece or the hands-free Bluetooth system in a car. When you turn the switch on, you're offered the chance to pair the iPhone with other Bluetooth equipment. See page 68 for step-by-step instructions.

- **Keyboard.** Here, you can turn *Auto-Capitalization* on or off. That's when you're entering text and the iPhone thoughtfully capitalizes the first letter of every new sentence for you.

  Enable Caps Lock is the on/off switch for the Caps Lock feature, in which a fast double-tap on the Shift key turns on Caps Lock (page 21).

- **Reset.** On the Reset screen, you'll find four ways to erase your tracks. *Reset All Settings* takes all of the iPhone's settings back to the way they were when it came from Apple. Your data, music, and videos remain in place, but the settings you've changed all go back to their factory settings.

  Erase All Content and Settings is the one you want when you sell your iPhone, or when you're captured by the enemy and want to make sure they will learn nothing from you or your iPhone.

  Reset Keyboard Dictionary has to do with the iPhone's autocorrection feature, which kicks in whenever you're trying to input text (page 25).

Ordinarily, every time you type something the iPhone doesn't recognize—some name or foreign word, for example—and you don't accept
the iPhone's suggestion, it adds the word you typed to its built-in dictionary so it doesn't bother you again with a suggestion the next time. If you
feel you've confused the dictionary by entering too many words that
aren't legitimate terms, you can delete from its little brain all of the new
words you've "taught" it.

Reset Network Settings makes the iPhone forget all of the memorized
Wi-Fi networks that it currently auto-recognizes.

Mail

On this page of settings, you set up your email account information, specify
how often you want the iPhone to check for new messages, change the font
size for email, and more.

- **Accounts.** You set up your email accounts here. See page 136 for details.

- **Messages.** How often do you want the iPhone to query the network to
  see if new mail is waiting for you? That's the purpose of the *Auto-Check*
  option. Tap it to choose *Every hour, Every 30 minutes, Every 15 minutes,* or

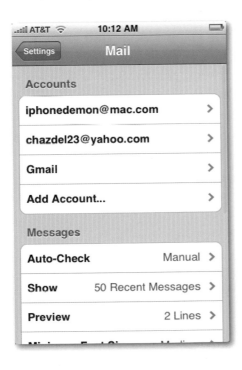

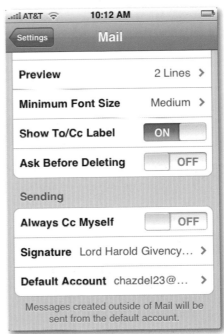

Manual (that is, only when you tap the Check button in the Mail program). Keep in mind that frequent checking means faster battery drain.

 The iPhone always checks email each time you open the Mail program, regardless of your setting here.

Using the *Show__ Recent Messages* option, you can limit how much mail the Mail program shows you, from the most recent 25 messages to the most recent 200. This feature doesn't limit you from getting and seeing all your mail—you can always tap Download More in the Mail program— but it may help to prevent the sinking feeling of Email Overload.

- **Preview.** It's very cool that the iPhone shows you the first few lines of text in every message. Here, you can specify how many lines of that preview text appear. More means you can skim your inbound mail without having to open many of them; less means that more messages fit on each screen without scrolling.

- **Minimum Font Size.** Anyone with fading vision—those of us over 40 know who we are—will appreciate this option. It lets you scale the type size of your email from Small to Giant.

- **Show To/Cc Label.** If you turn this option on, a tiny, light gray logo appears next to many of the messages in your In box. The **To** logo indicates that this message was addressed directly to you; the **Cc** logo means that you were merely "copied" on a message that was primarily intended for someone else.

  If there's no logo at all, then the message is in some other category. Maybe it came from a mailing list, or it's an email blast (a BCC), or the message is from you, or it's a bounced email message.

- **Ask before deleting.** Ordinarily, you can delete an email message fast and easily (page 146). If you'd prefer to see an "Are you sure?" confirmation box before the message disappears forever, turn this option on.

 The confirmation box appears only when you're deleting an open message—not when you delete one from the list of messages.

- **Always Cc Myself.** If this option is on, then you'll get a copy of any message you send; see page 141 for the rationale.

- **Signature.** A signature, of course, is a bit of text that gets stamped at the bottom of your outgoing email messages. Here's where you can change yours; see page 153 for details.

- **Default account.** Your iPhone can check a virtually unlimited number of email accounts. On this screen, you tap the name of the account you want to be your default account—that is, the one that's used whenever you compose a new message.

Phone

These settings have to do with your address book, call management, and other phone-related preferences.

- **My Number.** Gotta love the way the iPhone makes it so easy to find your own phone number. It's right here (as well as at the top of the Contacts list).

- **International Assist.** When this option is turned on, and when you're dialing from another country, the iPhone automatically adds the proper country codes when dialing U.S. numbers.

- **Sort Order, Display Order.** The question is: How do you want the names in your Contacts list sorted—by first name or last name?

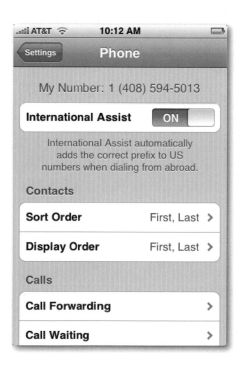

Note that you can have them sorted one way, but displayed another way. This table shows all four combinations of settings (the boldface shows you how they're sorted):

	Display "Last, First"	Display "First, Last"
Sort order "First, Last"	O'Furniture, Patty Minella, Sal Peace, Warren	Patty O'Furniture Sal Minella Warren Peace
Sort order "Last, First"	Minella, Sal O'Furniture, Patty Peace, Warren	Sal Minella Patty O'Furniture Warren Peace

As you can see, not all of these combinations make any sense.

- **Call Forwarding.** Tap to open the Call Forwarding screen, where you can turn this feature on or off. See page 67 for details.

- **Call Waiting.** Call Waiting, of course, is the feature that produces an audible beep, when you're on a phone call, to let you know that someone else is calling you. (Page 65 has details on how to handle such a traffic jam.)

  If Call Waiting is turned off, then such incoming calls go directly to voicemail.

- **Show My Caller ID.** Ordinarily, other people can see who's calling even before they answer the phone, thanks to the Caller ID display on their cellphones or some landline phones. If you'd feel more private by hiding your own number, so that people don't know who's calling until they answer your call, turn this feature off.

- **TTY.** A TTY (teletype) machine lets people with hearing or speaking difficulties use a telephone—by typing back and forth, or sometimes with the assistance of a human TTY operator who transcribes what the other person is saying.

  When you turn this iPhone option on, you can use the iPhone with a TTY machine, if you buy the little $20 iPhone TTY adapter from Apple.

- **Change Voicemail Password.** When you set up your AT&T account, you created a numeric password that's required to access your voicemail by dialing in. Ordinarily, you don't need this password, since Visual Voicemail (page 53) brings the messages right to your iPhone without your having to call in. But if you access your voicemail from other phones, here's where you can make up a new password. You'll be asked to enter your old one first.

- **SIM PIN.** As noted on page 8, your SIM card stores all your account information. SIM cards are especially desirable overseas, because in most countries, you can pop yours into any old phone and have working service. If you're worried about yours getting stolen or lost, turn this option on. You'll be asked to enter a password code.

  Then, if some bad guy ever tries to put your SIM card into another phone, he'll be asked for the password. Without the password, the card (and the phone) won't make calls.

> **Tip** And if the evildoer guesses wrong three times, the words "PIN LOCKED" appear on the screen, and the SIM card is locked forever. You'll have to get another one from AT&T. So don't forget the password.

- **AT&T Services.** Opens up a cheat sheet of handy numeric codes that, when dialed, play the voice of a robot providing useful information about your account. For example, *225# lets you know the latest status of your bill, *646# lets you know how many airtime minutes you've used so far this month, and so on.

> **Tip** The "AT&T My Account" button at the bottom of the screen opens up your account page on the Web, for further details on your cellphone billing and features.

Safari

Here's everything you ever wanted to adjust in the Web browser but didn't know how to ask.

- **JavaScript.** JavaScript is a programming language whose bits of code frequently liven up Web pages. If you suspect some bit of code is choking Safari, however, you can turn off its ability to decode JavaScript here.
- **Plug-ins.** Plug-ins offer another way to expand a Web browser's abilities, often by teaching it how to play certain formats of audio or video. Safari comes with a couple of basic ones—to play certain QuickTime movies on the Web, for example. There's not much point to turning them off in

the iPhone's version of Safari—there's no security risk, since you can't install any new ones—but it's here as a familiar option.

- **Block Pop-ups.** In general, you want this turned on. You really don't want pop-up ad windows ruining your surfing session. Now and again, though, pop-up windows are actually useful. When you're buying concert tickets, for example, a pop-up window might show the location of the seats. In that situation, you can turn this option off.

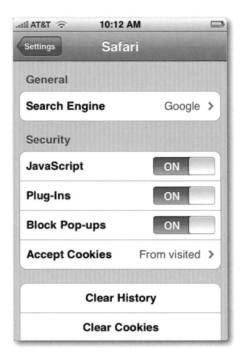

- **Accept Cookies.** Cookies are the tiny preference files that Web sites leave on your computer, usually to remember who you are. As described on page 132, these options let you limit how many are deposited on your iPhone.

- **Clear History.** Like any Web browser, Safari keeps a list of Web sites you've visited recently to make it easier for you to revisit them: the History list. And like any browser, Safari therefore exposes your tracks to any suspicious spouse or crackpot colleague who feels like investigating what you've been up to. If you're nervous about that prospect, tap Clear History to erase your tracks.

- **Clear Cookies,** similarly, deletes all the cookies that Web sites have deposited on your "hard drive."

- **Clear Cache.** See page 259.

iPod

On this panel, you can adjust four famous iPod playback features:

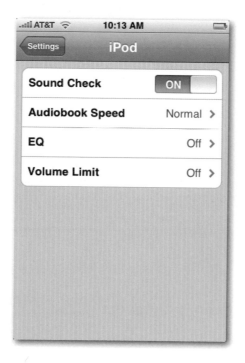

- **Sound Check** is a standard iPod feature that attempts to create a standard baseline volume level for the different songs in your library, so you don't crank up the volume to hear one song, and then get your eardrums turned to liquid by the next due to differences in CD mastering. Here's the on/off switch.

- **Audiobook Speed.** If you've bought audio books from Audible.com, you can take advantage of this feature to make the reader speed up a little or slow down a little—without sounding like either a chipmunk or James Earl Jones. (Your options are Slower, Normal, and Faster.)

- **EQ.** EQ is equalization—the art of fiddling with specific frequencies in your music to bring out highs, lows, midrange, or whatever, to suit certain types of music and certain musical tastes. This screen offers a scrolling list of predesigned EQ "envelopes" designed for different situations: Bass Booster, Hip-Hop, Small Speakers, Spoken Word, Treble Reducer, and so on. You can also choose Off, if you want the music to play just the way the record company released it.

- **Volume Limit.** It's well established that listening to loud music for a long time can damage your hearing. It's also well established that parents worry about this phenomenon. So all iPods, and the iPhone, include an optional, password-protected maximum-volume control. The idea is that if you give your kid an iPhone (wow, what a generous parent!), you can set a maximum volume level, using the slider on this screen.

  If you do adjust this slider, you're also asked for a four-digit password, to prevent your kid from bypassing your good intentions and dragging the slider right back to maximum. (The password isn't especially hard to bypass.)

 Needless to say, the risk of hearing damage exists only when you're wearing iPhone earbuds. Music pumped through the tiny speaker wouldn't damage a gnat's hearing.

Photos

All of the options here govern the behavior of the photo slideshows described on page 95.

- **Play Each Slide For.** How long do you want each photo to remain on the screen? You can choose 2, 3, 5, 10, or 20 seconds. (Hint: 2 is plenty, 3 at most. Anything more than that will bore your audience silly.)

- **Transition.** These options are visual effects between slides: various cross-fades, wipes, and other transitions.

- **Repeat, Shuffle.** These options work just as they do for music. *Repeat* makes the slideshow loop endlessly; *Shuffle* plays the slides in random order.

A Setup and Signup

The iPhone stands out from most cellphones in plenty of ways—no buttons, all touch screen, gigabytes of memory. But one of the most radical differences is the way you sign up for your cellular service. It's not in a phone store with a salesperson breathing down your neck. It's at home on your computer, in iTunes, where you can take all the time you need to read about the plans and choose the one you want.

The signup process pretty much explains itself. But it's worth noting a few twists and turns you'll meet along the way.

All of this, by the way, requires iTunes 7.3 or later. (See page 195 for details on getting this software for Mac or Windows.) To get started, put the iPhone into its cradle, and plug that into your computer. iTunes opens automatically, ready to begin.

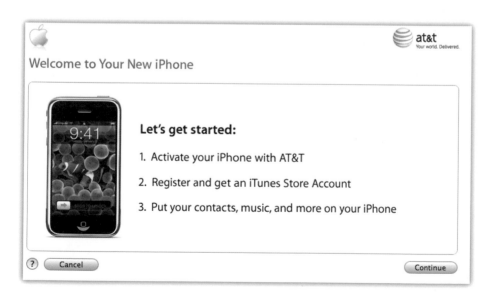

Activation, Step by Step

Activation means signing up for a plan, turning on the service, and either finding out your new phone number or transferring your old number to the iPhone.

Until you activate, the iPhone can't do much of anything. It can't make calls, play music or video, or get on the Internet. So no, you can't buy an iPhone and hope to use it as a fancy iPod: Without an AT&T account, it just won't work. Signing up for AT&T service is required.

For that matter, the iPhone is a *locked* GSM phone, meaning that it works *only* with an AT&T account. It won't work with Verizon, Sprint, T-Mobile, or any other carrier, and you can't insert the SIM card (page 8) from a non-AT&T phone and expect it to work.

Here are the screens you'll encounter as you click Continue to work your way through the signup process:

- **Welcome to Your New iPhone.** Aww, isn't that nice?

- **Are You a New or Existing AT&T (Cingular) Wireless Customer?** If you're already an AT&T or Cingular customer, clicking *Replace a phone on my account with this iPhone* lets you transfer your old phone number and calling plan to the iPhone. You'll just have to pay $20 more a month for the iPhone's unlimited Internet service.

  Click *Add a new line to my existing account* if you intend to keep your old phone as a backup, but add the iPhone.

  If you're not already with AT&T/Cingular, click *Activate one iPhone now* to get your new iPhone signed up. To activate more than one iPhone—for example, to get one of AT&T's family plans and get additional phones for your spouse and kids at a huge discount—click *Activate two or more iPhones on an Individual or FamilyTalk plan*.

- **Transfer Your Mobile Number?** You can bring your old cellphone or home phone number to your new iPhone. All your friends and coworkers can keep dialing your old number—but your iPhone will now ring instead of the old phone.

If that's what you want, fill in the blanks. It usually takes under an hour for a cellphone number transfer to take place—but it may take several hours. During that time, you can make calls on the iPhone, but can't receive them. (At least you didn't sign up for this service the first weekend that the iPhone was available, when it sometimes took 30 hours for the swamped AT&T computers to process the number transfers!)

 Note Transferring a landline number can take several *days*.

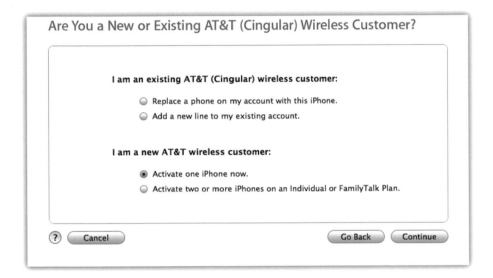

If you're not transferring an existing phone number, just ignore this screen and click Continue.

- **Select Your Monthly AT&T Plan.** Here's where you can read about the various monthly plans.

All of them include unlimited Internet use, 200 text messages a month, and unlimited calling to and from other AT&T phones. All of them also offer Rollover Minutes, which is something no other carrier offers. That is, if you don't use up all of your monthly minutes this month, the unused ones are automatically added to your allotment for next month, and so on.

All but the cheapest plan also offer unlimited calls on nights and weekends. The primary difference between the plans, therefore, is the number of weekday calling minutes you get.

Apple lists the three plans it considers the most mainstream—sort of a Good/Better/Best menu—but there are bigger plans available. You can upgrade your allotment of text messages (1,500 a month for $10, for example) or the number of minutes (click More Minutes). The heavy-talker plans range from $80 a month (1,350 weekday minutes) to $200 (6,000 minutes).

> **Tip** The choice you make here isn't etched in stone. You can change your plan at any time. At *www.wireless.att.com*, you can log in with your iPhone number and make up a password. Click My Account, and then click Change Rate Plan to view your options.

Select Your Monthly AT&T Plan

①		$59.99	$79.99	$99.99
Minutes		450	900	1350
Unlimited Data (Email/Web)		✓	✓	✓
Visual Voicemail		✓	✓	✓
SMS Text Messages		200	200	200

All iPhone plans require a two-year commitment and a $36 "activation fee" (ha!).

As you budget for your plan, keep in mind that, as with any cellphone, you'll also be paying taxes as high as 22 percent, depending on your state. Ouch.

- **iTunes Account (Apple ID).** If you've ever bought anything from Apple or the iTunes store, then you already have an Apple ID. Type your email address and password here. If you don't yet have an Apple ID, you'll need one to sign up for iPhone service. If you click Continue without filling in any blanks here, a series of screens will guide you through the creation of an iTunes account (Apple ID).

- **Customer Information for Apple and AT&T.** This screen might have been better titled "Miscellaneous." On it, you input your birthday (to prove that you're over 18), and you can turn on two checkboxes that land you on the Apple and AT&T email lists (so you can receive all kinds of exciting new junk mail).

- **Billing Information.** AT&T will send your cellphone bills to the address you supply.

And why does AT&T ask for your Social Security number? The same reason any cellphone carrier does when you sign up: so it can run a credit check to make sure you're a worthy credit risk.

If you're uncomfortable sending your Social Security number over the Internet, you can also stop in at an AT&T store, provide it to a salesperson there, and return home with a "credit-check code," which you then plug into this screen. The truth is, though, that the Social Security number is *less* likely to fall into the wrong hands if you send it over the Internet because iTunes encrypts it to keep it secure. You can't say that about the human AT&T salesperson who types your Social Security number into a computer to generate the check code.

If you don't pass the online credit check, you can write a check at an AT&T store. In that situation, too, you'll get a credit-check code to plug into this screen.

 Tip It's at this point that you could sign up for one of AT&T's pay-as-you-go plans. The drawback is that these are very expensive. The beauty is that you can cancel at any time, leaving your iPhone incapable of making calls but fully operational as an iPod and Wi-Fi Internet machine. (It's true! See page 267.)

- **Accept iPhone Terms & Conditions; Accept AT&T Service Agreement.** Gotta keep those lawyers occupied somehow.

- **Review Your Information.** You're getting one last look at all the information you've provided so far.

- **Completing Activation.** Here's where you find out what your new iPhone's phone number will be (if you didn't transfer your existing number). That's one downside of signing up for service at home: You can't ask for a couple of different phone-number options and choose the easiest one to remember.

Tip While you wait for your phone to be activated, it's not completely useless. You can still drag playlists from the iTunes Source list directly onto the iPhone's icon to get some music onto it.

You still can't access the iPhone's onscreen controls, of course—but you can use the earbud clicker to play, pause, and skip to the next song. Just something to keep you occupied until the activation is complete.

Once you make it through all the previous steps, you return to the regularly scheduled world of iTunes for two final bits of administrative business:

- **Set Up Your iPhone.** Here's where you get to name your iPhone. Your iPhone's icon will bear this name each time you sync. You can always change it later in iTunes by double-clicking the same icon.

    You also get your first (but not last) opportunity to turn off the automatic syncing feature that makes loading up your iPhone so effortless. See page 208 for details.

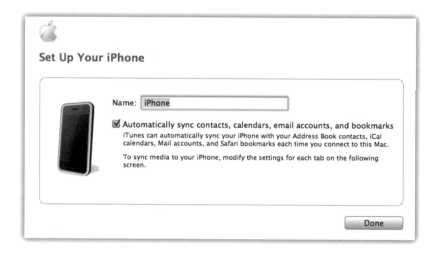

- **Your iPhone contains diagnostic information.** The iPhone keeps internal logs of crashes, restarts, and other glitchiness. If you give your permission on this screen, the phone will transmit these logs to Apple—*without* any identifying information like your name. The idea is that its engineers, when studying the collected, aggregated glitch data from thousands of anonymous people, will be better able to spot trends, debug the thing, and issue a software update that improves stability.

And that's the ball game. You now arrive on the main iTunes screen, with the six iPhone tabs across the top: Music, Podcasts, Videos, and so on. Now you can specify what you want copied onto the phone. Turn to Chapter 11 for details.

Pay-As-You-Go Plans

Most people assume that a two-year AT&T commitment is required, possibly because Apple says, "two-year AT&T commitment required." That's not technically true, however.

If you enter 999-99-9999 as your Social Security number and click Continue, you'll fail the credit check. And what happens to people who fail the credit check?

They're offered the chance to sign up for one of AT&T's *GoPhone* plans. These are prepaid plans, intended for people with poor credit (or a fear of commitment). You pay for each month's service in advance, and it's very expensive: $60 a month buys you only 300 minutes, for example.

But here's the thing: There's no two-year commitment, no deposit, no contract. You can stop paying at any time without having to pay the usual $175 early-termination fee.

In fact, if you remove the SIM card at that point, the Wi-Fi and iPod features of the iPhone still work. If you really want an Internet terminal/iPod that can't make phone calls, or if you can afford an iPhone but not an AT&T service plan, well, here's your chance.

 Tip Clearly, this business about using the iPhone without an AT&T plan is something of a loophole—and Apple/AT&T may eventually close it. Caveat hacker.

B Troubleshooting and Maintenance

The iPhone is a computer, and you know what that means. Things can go wrong. This particular computer, though, is not quite like a Mac, a PC, or a Treo. It's brand new. It runs a spin-off of the Mac OS X operating system, but that doesn't mean you can troubleshoot it like a Mac. There's no collected wisdom, no massive list of Web sites filled with troubleshooting tips and anecdotal suggestions.

Until there is, this chapter will have to be your guide when things go wrong.

First Rule: Install the Updates

There's an old saying that's more true than ever: "Never buy version 1.0 of anything."

The very first version of anything has bugs, glitches, and things the programmers didn't have time to finish they way they would have liked. The iPhone is no exception.

The beauty of this phone, though, is that Apple can send it fixes, patches, and even new features through software updates. One day you'll connect the phone to your computer for charging or syncing, and—bam!—there'll be a note from iTunes that new iPhone software is available.

So the first rule of trouble-free iPhoning is to accept these updates when they're offered. With each new software blob, Apple removes another few dozen tiny glitches.

Reset: Six Degrees of Desperation

The iPhone runs actual programs, and as actual programs, they actually crash. Sometimes, the program you're working in simply vanishes and you find yourself back at the Home screen. (That can happen when, for example, Safari encounters some plug-in or data type on a Web page that it doesn't know how to handle.) Just reopen the program and get on with your life.

If the program you're in just doesn't seem to be working right—it's frozen or acting weird, for example—one of the following six resetting techniques usually clears things right up.

 Note Proceed down this list in order! Start with the easy ones.

- **Force-quit the program.** On an iPhone, you're never aware that you're "launching" and "exiting" programs. They're always just *there*, like TV channels, when you switch to them. But if a program locks up or acts glitchy, you can *force* it to quit. Hold down the Home key for six seconds.

  The next time you open that program from the Home screen, it should be back in business.

- **Turn the phone off and on again.** Try this one next if it seems something more serious has gone wrong. Hold down the Sleep/Wake switch for three seconds. When the screen says, "slide to power off," confirm by swiping. The iPhone shuts off completely.

  Turn it back on by tapping the Sleep/Wake switch.

- **Reset the phone's hardware.** And what if the phone is locked up so badly that you can't even turn it off? Then you'll have to shut it off by force. To do that, hold the Home button *and* the Sleep/Wake button for eight seconds, or until the Apple logo appears. The phone turns off, all right!

- **Reset the phone's settings.** Relax. Resetting doesn't erase any of your data—only the phone's settings. From the Home screen, tap Settings→General→Reset→Reset All Settings.

- **Erase the whole phone.** From the Home screen, tap Settings→General→Reset→Erase All Content and Settings. Now *this* option zaps all

your stuff—all of it. Music, videos, email, all gone. Clearly, you're getting into last resorts here.

- **Restore the phone.** If none of these steps seem to solve the phone's glitchiness, it might be time for the Nuclear Option: Erasing it completely, resetting both hardware and software back to factory-fresh condition.

> **Tip** If you're able to sync the phone with iTunes *first*, do it! That way, you'll have a backup of all those intangible iPhone data bits: text messages, call logs, Recents list, and so on. iTunes will put it all back onto the phone the first time you sync after the restore.

To restore the phone, connect it to your computer. In iTunes, click the iPhone icon and then, on the Summary tab, click Restore. Confirm this drastic decision.

When it's all over, you can sync your life right back onto the iPhone—this time, if the technology gods are smiling, with better success.

iPhone

Name: MyPhone
Capacity: 7.27 GB
Software Version: 1.0
Serial Number: YM7230PXWH8
Phone Number: 1 (203) 216-3468

Version

Your iPhone software is up to date. iTunes will automatically check for an update again on 7/17/07.

[Check for Update]

If you are experiencing problems with your iPhone, you can restore its original settings by clicking Restore.

[Restore]

iPhone Doesn't Show Up in iTunes

If the iPhone's icon doesn't appear in the Source list at the left side of the iTunes window, you've got yourself a real problem. You won't be able to load it up with music, videos, or photos, and you won't be able to sync it with your computer. That's a bad thing.

- **The USB factor.** Trace the connection from the iPhone, to its cradle, to the USB cable, to the computer, making sure everything is seated. Also, don't plug the USB cable into a USB jack on your keyboard, and don't plug it into an unpowered USB hub.

- **The iPhone factor.** Try turning the phone off and on again. Make sure it's got a battery charge.

- **The iTunes factor.** The iPhone won't show up in versions of iTunes earlier than 7.3. Download and install the latest. No success? Then reinstall it.

Battery Won't Fully Charge

When the battery is fully charged, the lightning-bolt icon on the battery icon (top of the screen) changes into a little plug icon. You should be ready to head out into the world, with your own world in your pocket. Unless, of course, you never *see* the plug icon.

Turns out this is a software bug, not a battery bug. Your battery is fully charged—it's just that the status-bar icon never shows the little happy plug. Apple fixed this problem in its first iPhone software update.

Phone and Internet Problems

What can go wrong with the phone part of the iPhone? Let us count the ways.

- **Can't make calls.** First off, do you have enough AT&T cellular signal to make a call? Check your signal-strength bars. Even if you have one or two, flakiness is par for the course. Try going outside, standing near a window, or moving to a major city. (Kidding.)

  Also, make sure Airplane mode isn't turned on (page 110). Try calling somebody else, to make sure the problem isn't with the number you're dialing.

  If nothing else works, try the resetting techniques described at the beginning of this chapter.

- **Can't get on the Internet.** Remember, the iPhone can get online in two ways: via Wi-Fi hot spot and via AT&T's EDGE network. If you're not in a hot spot *and* you don't have an EDGE signal—that is, if neither the .ıll nor the E icon appears at the top of the screen—then you can't get online at all.

  And, of course, you can't get online when you've got Airplane mode turned on.

- **Can't receive text messages.** If your buddies try to send you text messages that contain picture or video attachments, you'll never see them (the messages, that is, not the buddies). Ask your correspondents to email them to you instead.

- **Can't send text messages.** Make sure the recipient's phone number in Contacts has an area code.

- **"Could not activate EDGE" messages.** This message just means that the iPhone has tried to get online—to check email on a schedule you've established, for example—but couldn't get onto AT&T's cellular data network. Usually, the AT&T signal is too weak or there's a temporary outage in your area. In any case, one thing's for sure: If you wait long enough, this message will go away.

Can't Send Email

It's happened to thousands of people. You set up your POP email account (page 136), and everything looks good. But although you can *receive* mail, you can't *send* it. You create an outgoing message, you tap Send. The whirlygig "I'm thinking" cursor spins and spins, but the iPhone never sends the message.

The problem's cause is very technical, but here's a nicely oversimplified explanation.

When you send a piece of postal mail, you might drop it off at the post office. It's then sent over to the *addressee's* post office in another town, and delivered from there.

In a high-tech sort of way, the same thing happens with email. When you send a message, it goes first to your Internet provider's *email server* (central mail computer). It's then sent to the *addressee's* mail server, and the addressee's email program picks it up from there.

But spammers and spyware writers became an increasing nuisance, especially people who wrote *zombies*—spyware on your computer that churns out spam without your knowledge. So the big ISPs (Internet service providers) began fighting back in two ways—both of which can block outgoing mail from your iPhone, too. Here's the scoop:

- **Use port 587.** *Ports* are invisible "channels" from a computer to the Internet. One conducts email, one conducts Web activity, and so on. Most computers send email out on port 25.

  In an effort to block zombie spam, though, the big ISPs have rigged their networks so that mail you send from port 25 can go only to one place: the ISPs' own mail servers. (Most zombies attempt to send mail directly to the *addressees'* mail servers, so they're effectively blocked.) Your iPhone tries to send mail on port 25—and it gets blocked.

  The solution? Choose a different port. From the Home screen, tap Settings→Mail. Tap the name of your POP account. Scroll down to the Outgoing Mail Server. Tap the address there to edit it. Whatever's there, add *:587* to the end of it. So *mail.ixmail.com* becomes *mail.ixmail.com:587*.

  Try sending mail again. If it's still not sending, try changing that suffix to *:465*.

- **Use AT&T's mail server.** When you're home, your computer is connected directly, via cable modem or DSL, to the Internet provider's network. It knows you and trusts you.

But when you're out and about, and your iPhone uses AT&T's cellular EDGE network (Chapter 6), your Internet provider doesn't recognize you. Your email is originating *outside* your ISP's network—and it gets blocked. For all the ISP knows, you're a spammer.

Your ISP may have a special mail-server address that's just for people to use while they're traveling. But the simpler solution may just be to use AT&T's *own* mail-server address. Tap Settings→Mail→the name of your POP account→Outgoing Mail Server. Tap the address there to edit it. Replace whatever's there with *cwmx.com* (which, at one time, stood for Cingular Wireless Mail Exchange).

If you're like thousands of people, that simple change means you can now send messages when you're on AT&T's network and not just receive them.

Problems That Aren't Really Problems

There's a difference between "things not working as they were designed to" and "things not working the way I'd like them to work." Here are a few examples:

- **Rotation sensor doesn't work.** As you know, the screen image is supposed to rotate into horizontal mode when you turn the iPhone itself. But this feature works only in Safari and when viewing photos, not in any other program.

  Furthermore, the iPhone has to be more or less upright when you turn it. It can't be flat on a table, for example. The orientation sensor relies on gravity to tell it which way you're holding the phone.

- **I hear only the audio of my video podcasts!** Actually, it's a feature, not a bug. You can listen to the audio of your video podcasts if you access them from one of the iPod program's *audio* lists (like Songs). To see the video, open the podcast from within the Videos list.

- **The phone volume is low—even the speakerphone.** That's true. The iPhone's ringer, earpiece, and speaker aren't as loud as on some other phones. (P.S.—With all due respect: did you remove the plastic film from your brand-new iPhone? This plastic, intended to be on the phone only during shipping, covers up the earpiece.)

 Tip The speaker volume is a lot better when it's pointed at you, either on a table or with your hand cupped around the bottom of the phone to direct the sound.

- **My fancy headphones don't fit the jack.** That's because the iPhone's headphone jack is recessed. See page 239.

- **I can't send a text message to more than one person, attach more than one photo to an email message, or copy and paste text.** The iPhone doesn't let you do any of it. Bummer.

- **My Notes don't sync back to my computer!** True. But the army of iPhone geeks has come up with an ingenious solution—don't use Notes for your notes. Instead, use the Note field in Contacts!

  To do so, create a new Contact and name it, say, *To Do list*. To this otherwise empty Contact, add a Notes field and fill it up. From now on, you'll find that note on your computer, filed under the proper name.

 Tip If your computer's address book program lets you set up contact *groups,* create one called Notes to hold all of these fake memo contacts.

iPod Problems

The iPhone is a great iPod, but even here, things can go wrong.

- **Can't hear anything.** Are the earbuds plugged in? They automatically cut the sound coming from the iPhone's built-in speaker.

  Is the volume up? Press the Up volume key on the side of the phone. Also make sure that the music is, in fact, supposed to be playing (and isn't on Pause).

- **Can't sync music or video files to the iPhone.** They may be in a format the iPhone doesn't understand, like WMA, MPEG-1, MPEG-2, or Audible Format 1.

  Convert them first to something the iPhone does understand, like AAC, Apple Lossless, MP3, WAV, Audible Formats 2, 3, or 4, AIFF (these are all audio formats), and H.264 or MPEG-4 (video formats).

- **Something not playing or syncing right.** It's technically possible for some corrupted or incompatible music, photo, or video file to jam up the entire syncing or playback process. In iTunes, experiment with playlists and videos, turning off checkboxes until you figure out which one is causing the problem.

Warranty and Repair

The iPhone comes with a one-year warranty. If you buy an AppleCare contract ($80), you're covered for a second year.

 Tip AT&T tech support is free for both years of your contract. They handle questions about your iPhone's phone features.

If, during the coverage period, anything goes wrong that's not your fault, Apple will fix it free. You can either take in the phone to an Apple store, which is often the fastest route, or call 800-APL-CARE (800 275-2273) to arrange shipping back to Apple. In general, you'll get the fixed phone back in three business days.

 Note *Sync the phone before it goes in for repair.* The repair process generally erases everything on the phone.

Also, don't forget to remove your SIM card (page 9) before you send in your broken iPhone—and to put it back in when you get the phone. Don't leave it in the loaner phone. AT&T will help you get a new card if you lose your original, but it's a hassle.

While your phone is in the shop, you can sign up for a loaner iPhone to use in the meantime for $30. Apple will ship it to you, or you can pick one up at the Apple store. Just sync this loaner phone with iTunes, and presto—all of your stuff is right back on it.

You can keep this service phone until seven days after you get your fixed phone back.

Out-of-Warranty Repairs

Once the year or two has gone by, Apple charges $200 or $250 to repair an iPhone (for the 4 and 8-gigabyte models).

The Battery Replacement Program

Why did Apple seal the battery inside the iPhone, anyway? Everyone knows that lithium-ion batteries don't last forever. After 300 or 400 charges, the iPhone battery will begin to hold less charge (perhaps 80 percent of the original). After a certain point, the phone will need a new battery. How come you can't change it yourself, as on any normal cellphone?

Conspiracy theorists have all kinds of ideas: It's a plot to generate service fees. It's a plot to make you buy a new phone. It's Steve Jobs's design aesthetic on crack.

The truth is more mundane: a user-replaceable battery takes up a lot more space inside the phone. It requires a plastic compartment that shields the guts of the phone from you and your fingers; it requires a removable door; and it needs springs or clips to hold the battery in place. All of this would mean either a much smaller battery—or a much bulkier phone. (As an eco-bonus, Apple properly disposes of the old batteries, which consumers might not do on their own.)

In any case, you can't change the battery yourself. If the phone is out of warranty, you must send it to Apple (or take it to an Apple store) for an $85 battery-replacement job.

Battery-Life Tips

The biggest wolfers of electricity on your iPhone are its screen and its wireless features. Therefore, you can get substantially longer life from each battery charge by using these features:

- **Dim the screen.** In bright light, the screen brightens (but uses more battery power); in dim light, it darkens.

  The screen adjusts with the help of an ambient light sensor that's hiding behind the glass above the earpiece.

  You can use this information to your advantage. By covering up the sensor as you unlock the phone, you force it to a low-power, dim screen setting (because the phone believes that it's in a dark room). Or by holding it up to a light as you wake it, you get full brightness. In both cases, you've saved all the taps and navigation it would have taken you to find the manual brightness slider in Settings.

 Note Apple tried having the light sensor active all the time, but it was weird to have the screen constantly dimming and brightening as you used it. So the sensor now samples the ambient light, and adjusts the brightness, only once—when you unlock the phone after waking it.

- **Turn off the radios.** The iPhone has *three* radios: one each for AT&T's cellular service, Wi-Fi Internet, and Bluetooth. You can turn off all three of them in one fell swoop by turning on Airplane mode (page 110). Do that whenever it's practical. You'll get a *lot* more life out of each charge.

You can also leave the phone on and turn off Wi-Fi and Bluetooth as needed; they're both in Settings.

- **At least turn off Wi-Fi searching.** Tap Home→Settings→Wi-Fi→On/Off. If you're not in a wireless hot spot anyway, you may as well stop the thing from using its radio. Or, at the very least, tell the iPhone to stop *searching* for Wi-Fi networks it can connect to (page 108). That's a big battery drain. Just connect manually when you know you're in a hot spot (page 108).

- **Cool your email's jets.** An iPhone that's set to check for new mail every 15 minutes (page 141) will drain the battery faster than one that checks every hour.

- **Use it sometimes.** The battery likes at least a little exercise. Make sure the battery is drained and recharged at least once a month.

- **Turn off equalization (EQ).** Audio EQ is designed to enhance certain frequencies for certain tastes and types of music (page 86). If you can get by without it, turn it off, both on the iPhone (Settings→iPod→EQ) and in iTunes, because processing the audio in real time stresses the iPhone's processor and thereby eats up battery power.

Index

L

light sensor, 10, 27
locked mode
  status icon, 11
looping, 80
loupe, 23-24

M

magnifying glass (loupe), 23-24
Mail *see* **email**
Mail (Mac)
  syncing email accounts, 225
making calls, 29-31, 50-52 *see also* **Contact list; Favorites list; Recents list**
  overseas calling, 50-52
maps, 175-184
  bookmarks, 180
  defined, 176
  driving directions, 181-182
  finding businesses, 178-179
  finding contacts, 178-179
  finding locations, 177-178
  location details, 179
  pinching and spreading, 18
  pushpins, 178-179
  Recents list, 180
  traffic alerts, 183-184
  zooming in/out, 176-177
microphone, 14-16
Microsoft Outlook
  syncing calendars, 223
  syncing contacts, 218
  syncing email accounts, 225
missingmanuals.com, 4
Mojits, 235
MojoDock, 235
Move and Scale screen, 100
mp3 files, 128-129
music playback
  bit rates, 199
  earbuds clicker, 32-33
  elapsed time, 80
  EQ (equalization), 86

  in the background, 81-82
  looping, 80
  Now Playing screen, 77-78
  On-The-Go playlist, 86-87
  shuffle mode, 80
  silencer switch, 12-13
  status icon, 11
  volume controls, 12-13
  volume slider, 79

N

Notes program, 193-194
  creating new, 193
  deleting, 194
  don't sync, 276
  emailing, 194
  keyboard, 20-26
number keys, 24-25 *see also* **keypad**

O

On-The-Go playlist
  creating, 86
  editing, 87
on/off switch, 6
options *see* **Settings program**
outlets *see* **AC adapter**
Outlook *see* **Microsoft Outlook**
Outlook Express
  syncing contacts, 218
  syncing email accounts, 225

P

padlock
  status icon, 11
Page Juggler, 129-131
  button, 115
Palm Desktop
  syncing contacts, 220
panning
  photos, 93
passcode lock, 250
pay-as-you-go plans, 267
period key, 24-25